Love Mercy

Love Mercy

Love Mercy

The Twelve Steps of Forgiveness

Samuel Wells

CANTERBURY
PRESS
Norwich

First published in 2020 by the Canterbury Press Norwich
Editorial office
3rd Floor, Invicta House
108–114 Golden Lane
London EC1Y 0TG, UK
www.canterburypress.co.uk

Canterbury Press is an imprint of Hymns Ancient & Modern
Ltd (a registered charity)

Hymns Ancient & Modern® is a registered trademark of
Hymns Ancient & Modern Ltd
13A Hellesdon Park Road, Norwich,
Norfolk NR6 5DR, UK

All rights reserved. No part of this publication may be
reproduced, stored in a retrieval system, or transmitted,
in any form or by any means, electronic, mechanical,
photocopying or otherwise, without the prior permission of
the publisher, Canterbury Press.

The Author has asserted his right under the Copyright,
Designs and Patents Act 1988 to be identified as the
Author of this Work

British Library Cataloguing in Publication data

A catalogue record for this book is available
from the British Library

978 1 78622 265 7

Typeset by Regent Typesetting

For Ray and Karen

Contents

Preface   ix

1 Become Resolved   1
2 Cease to Fight   11
3 Tell a Truthful Story   22
4 Say Sorry   33
5 Make Penance   42
6 Form an Agreement   50
7 Reach Repentance   59
8 Seek Mercy   67
9 Forgive   76
10 Be Reconciled   86
11 Be Healed   96
12 Be Raised   105

Preface

As I wrote *Walk Humbly*[1] I came to realize that it would be one of three books, which could be read in any order, or independently of one another. *Love Mercy* is intended to raise questions that *Walk Humbly* addresses, and to address questions that *Walk Humbly* raises. I trust these two books will in due course be joined by *Act Justly*, seeking likewise to deepen reflection and inspire engagement.

What follows is an exploration of twelve steps of peace. The process of making peace would normally need to include all these steps, but not necessarily in the same order as this book. That said, the steps are set out in this order for good reasons; and, more significantly, harm can be caused and the process may be inhibited if the later steps are ventured upon prematurely. Forgiveness comes near the end of the process, rather than near the beginning. To contemplate forgiveness, a number of prior steps need to be undertaken. Harm needs to cease. Truth needs to be told. Apology needs to be made. Trust needs to be established. Recompense needs to be attempted. There's no doubt forgiveness

---

1 Norwich: Canterbury Press, 2019.

can be an act of will or even habit; but if rushed, forgiveness may prove to have been based on fragile foundations and may later come to be regretted, withdrawn or recanted. Likewise, seeking reconciliation in the absence of major progress on the foregoing steps is like quelling a cry of rage without understanding its cause.

What this twelve-step model makes explicit are the specifically theological dimensions of the process. The model offers a way to distinguish between those steps generic to all forms of peacebuilding, and those that are distinctively Christian. Thus steps 1–6 require no explicit theological narration. That's not to say that they don't have potential theological dimensions; the first step, for example, is fundamentally about identity, and the fifth step, penance, has a long history as a Christian practice. But they make transparent sense outside the language of the church and the Christian story. By contrast, steps 7–10 are explicitly Christian notions, albeit ones that find parallels in other traditions. The fact, for example, that in more liturgical traditions confession usually comes near the beginning of the Eucharist, is a statement of an assumption that Christians are always in a process of making peace, and that reconciliation always involves us in naming and disentangling ourselves from our own complicity in provoking and promoting disorder. Steps 11–12 are different again: whereas 1–6 are prudent actions that Christians may see as being led by the Spirit, and 7–10 involve specific Christian practices that seek to imitate the ways of the Trinity, 11–12 are acts of God,

in which the Holy Spirit makes present the benefits
of Christ's ministry. They are signs that invite us to
glimpse on earth how things are in heaven; to enjoy a
foretaste of what God has prepared.

There are circumstances in which it's almost impossible to make any progress through the steps of this
peace process: for example when there's a huge dis-
parity of power and the powerful party is inflicting
regular hurt and damage upon another party without
provocation. In such a case, employing the language
for the second half of the process – forgiveness, for
example – is almost always wholly inappropriate. By
describing how a peace process works, and what are
the preconditions for it to work, I'm not suggesting
that it always works, or can always work.

In *Love Mercy* I've tried to stay within a triangle.
The first side of that triangle is the area of personal
experience. I'm seeking to touch on areas that may be
painful for the reader, because of broken relationships,
longstanding bitterness or abiding guilt. I want to get
to the heart of what's wrong, offer examples and strategies for a journey of healing, and reveal what such a
journey is really about.

I strive to retain the intensity of personal engagement. But on the second side of the triangle I'm seeking
to recognize structural injustice and systemic inequality. Personal antagonism is often a symptom of, and
subsumed within, a whole swathe of wrongs across
time and space. I try to cover a wide spectrum, from
the domestic and suburban to the catastrophic and
global, so everyone can identify with the argument.

The third side of the triangle is a form of emotional, philosophical and theological analysis and prescription. The argument is deliberately shaped so that theological concerns, which are latent at the start, gradually surface, gaining profile from Chapter 7 onwards, until in the last two chapters they suffuse the whole scene, and it becomes clear the argument was theological all along. In the final chapters I deliberately discuss particular scriptural passages in detail, because I want to demonstrate that the Bible is not a spiritual or pious text set apart from the thick of these practices. On the contrary, these steps and this agonizing journey are precisely what the Bible is about. The style is intended to be similar enough to *Walk Humbly* to be recognizable, but sufficiently different to be complementary, and thus to model the creative tension the whole argument is advocating.

In contrast to many treatments of forgiveness and reconciliation, what I haven't done is gather a great cloud of witnesses to attest to the power and wonder of such journeys. I don't disparage such stirring accounts, and have read and heard a good many in preparing this book; but I'm nervous of such a parade, both because it puts huge pressure on the protagonists to be exemplars, if not angels, and because every such account leaves you wondering whether you've really heard the whole story. What I've done instead is to attend to such narratives, try to distil the key moments and transferable truth at the heart of them, and then present those insights in a context that might stimulate and empower readers to become such an example themselves. At times I do tell stories, but these are either fiction or sufficiently stylized to be like fiction, and thus illuminate key steps without the reader becoming distracted by wanting to know what 'really happened'.

It doesn't occur to me that anyone will obediently and methodically follow this proposal, step by step. For those profoundly more sinned against than sinning, for example, Chapters 2, 4, 5, 7 and 8 might describe things they are looking for more in others than in themselves. But even then I hope those chapters will provide helpful insight into what they are actually expecting another party to do. Particular circumstances will shape how a journey of peace might proceed – for example, whether a series of face-to-face encounters, as envisaged at Chapter 10, is actually possible. In being succinct, I risk being regarded in some cases as inaccurate or insufficient. My proposal is intended as a humble gift, not a comprehensive or commandeering prescription.

There are those on whose ideas I have built my own, and thus without whom I might never have imagined writing such a book; among these are Ched Myers, Stanley Hauerwas and John Milbank. There are those whose example I revere; among these are Marcia Owen, John Inge, Mindy Makant, Helen Prejean and Jo Wells. There are many whose work, while not visible in mine, has nonetheless been fruitful in identifying what I wanted to say; among these are Desmond Tutu, Paul Ricoeur, Jacques Derrida, L. Gregory Jones, John Paul Lederach, Elaine Enns and Bryan Stevenson. And there are companions on the way. Charlene Kammerer invited me to give a lecture in which I first articulated the twelve steps. Jolyon Mitchell asked me to write a chapter in which I began to ponder what those twelve steps really meant. Jess White helped me greatly in delving into what luminaries had said on the subject and in appreciating the aforementioned cloud of witnesses. Maureen Knudsen Langdoc made helpful suggestions on the manuscript.

I write as one who has watched some tread this trail, has sought to accompany others on their journey, and who has humbly tried to walk this path himself. For those who have shown me costly grace and Christlike peace on those travels, this book is a modest token of recognition, and gratitude.

Become Resolved

Consider two kinds of relationships. In one, difference, tension and conflict are apparent, recognized and addressed. The second kind is intended to be a refuge from conflict – so special that difference can be transcended, or so casual that tension can be ignored.

A superficial, or sentimental, approach to relating to others understands the second kind as normal, and the first as a wearisome exception. In such a view there are intimates, from whom can be expected love, kindness and loyalty; there are regular acquaintances, such as neighbours and colleagues, customers and clients, and those paid for services, from whom can be expected civility and common decency; and there are strangers, who could conceivably become intimates or regular acquaintances, and could potentially be causes for tension, but who more likely can be largely ignored. If conflict arises with a stranger, it can be handled assertively but dispassionately – don't be ripped off, don't be trodden on, don't be racially or religiously abused, don't be treated like dirt – but above all, don't get too involved. If tensions arise with a regular acquaintance, it may not go away on its own: it may require sitting down over a drink or a coffee, it may involve an honest word or the drawing of a line in the sand, it may result in a parting of the professional ways; these things happen. But if differences surface in the group of intimates, it can be indescribably painful.

Why? Because a widespread yet sentimental definition assumes 'intimate' refers to 'one with whom I have no differences' – and the disclosure of difference not only disturbs the calm effortlessness of the relationship but questions the whole premise of intimacy. Thus when a difference arises with an intimate – perhaps the most intimate, a life partner – it triggers an existential crisis: am I to close down, deny and suppress difference in order to preserve my illusion that intimacy circumvents difference? Or do I have to enter a whole new world – a world in which every relationship (even with the stranger, and especially with the intimate) is an occasion for genuine, well-grounded and unavoidable tension, and life is the business of either naming and addressing those tensions, avoiding and suppressing them, or seeking by devious means to emerge victorious from countless undeclared wars?

That whole new world is what this book is about. It's a world in which every relationship evokes difference, tension and conflict. If these issues are ignored, they simply push engagements underground, where feelings fester, antagonism is perpetuated, and outcomes are achieved by underhand means. What does an outbreak of violence manifest? It demonstrates that more constructive ways of addressing tension have not been encouraged, fostered, or in some cases even attempted. Suppression of tension is the storing-up of explosive energy until a later, often less opportune moment of release. The kind of relationship in which difference, tension and conflict are apparent, recognized and addressed is a name for the whole new world that we enter when we realize how much of our lives we use up, energy we expend and sleep we lose suppressing, avoiding or trying surreptitiously to subvert conflict.

Conflict dominates people's lives. It takes over, most often despite people's best efforts to ignore it, avoid it or pretend it doesn't exist. For many, life is a concatenation of elaborate and extensive diversion strategies; indeed, that's the whole method of what I called above the second approach to relationships. But because these strategies deny the depth of the conflict and constantly attempt to distract from it, they never foster the skills and practices needed to resolve tension and make difference a source of creativity and energy rather than anger and bitterness. The result is that, striving to live without conflict, without the resources to address the tensions that inevitably arise, such tactics lead people into profound, intractable and bitter disputes, with no apparent way out. The tragedy is that such people are not a beleaguered minority: they are almost everybody.

But not quite everybody. Before going further, it's important to acknowledge that conflict can invigorate, energize and captivate. Competition, after all, is a qualified kind of conflict, in which combat is permitted and valorized within carefully established constraints. And competition, be it athletic, financial or aesthetic, constitutes a large part of many lives, the emotional beat of many souls, and a more-or-less healthy displacement of many feelings of hurt or frustration. Yet the spectre of the flaccid former sports star, the retired battle-hardened soldier or the bewildered emeritus executive vividly portrays the pathos of a life given over to competition when the heat of the contest is done. Such competition involves not just technical prowess but mental discipline, not just the facility of rising to a challenge but the ability to gain a psychological hold on the opposition, not just total emotional focus but a knack of finding extra impetus under pressure. While such attributes are vital for succeeding in the controlled environment of competition, where the purpose is limited and recognized, rules are accepted, and the goal explicit, they can be worse than useless in the uncontrolled context of interpersonal or corporate tension, where the battle is undeclared, the terms of engagement contested, and the goal far from clear.

How easy it is, then, to default to treating a conflict as a competition, in which winning is all, and a hand-shake afterwards reassures participants that it's only a game. But tension and conflict in life are not a game in this sense – of limited duration, with clear boundaries and accepted rules. Moreover this is a world where 'winning' – still less, being seen to win, with all the kudos and humiliation involved – is not a cause for celebration, because it perpetuates tension, exacerbates resentment and multiplies bitterness. In truth, competition, addictive as it becomes, compulsive as it may be, when wrongly employed, only amplifies conflict. Tension comes to infiltrate every aspect of life. It ultimately narrows, impoverishes and depletes.

It *narrows* because I reduce the focus of my life.
Rather than saying, 'The road is wide and the prospects
are splendid', I say, 'I am determined to destroy this
single enemy.' This single project obscures so many
other worthy goals and downgrades so many other
joyful enterprises. It *impoverishes* because I postpone
all other fulfilment. My imagination is mesmerized by
the bounty to be had through vanquishing my oppon-
ent. But this bounty turns out to have no abiding value:
it's the expense of spirit in a waste of shame. It *depletes*
because I mortgage the pursuit of virtue – the desire to
live an honourable, honest life – in order to fund the
pursuit of victory. But that victory is in a battle that
truly can have no winner. The perfect example of this
is the way compromise – a word whose origin lies in
making a promise together, building common trust – is
traduced into a forbidden betrayal, a path to hell.

What has become of me? That's the question that
begins the journey of peace. I've become a shadow of
my former self, a quivering mantis, bent on revenge,
shorn of humanity, kindness, humour, self-awareness,
decency. That's what the prodigal son, abject in humiliation, realized in the pigsty, and what his elder brother,
consumed by envy, failed to perceive in the field. To
emerge from conflict requires each party to perceive or
reassert a sense of its own respective identity that is not
subsumed within the conflict – a sense of purpose or
vocation that isn't locked into primal enmity with its
adversary. In vernacular terms, it's the moment when
a critical friend says, 'You're bigger than this', or 'You
may want to shoot them all, but they're not worth the

bullets.' Perhaps the best way to begin the conversation is to suggest, 'There are two people called Chris. One is the person I used to know – carefree, generous, interested in others, funny, lively; the other is the person you've become since this all started – short-tempered, obsessive, sleepless, anxious, twitchy. I'd like the old Chris back, please. Wouldn't you?'

The path to peace begins with a decision about identity. What kind of a person do I want to be? A person subject to the poison of this conflict, a prisoner of this fight, locked into the perpetual emotional labyrinths in which the pursuit of this addiction has entangled me? Or a person who has substituted the abundance of grace for the scarcity of combat, has reopened their life to the other as a gift rather than a threat, has perceived a future that's bigger than the past? Just as the key step in a twelve-step programme is to recognize our own powerlessness – that 'our lives have become unmanageable' and we are in the grip of addiction – so the first step to peace is to admit, 'My life is overwhelmed by this conflict; I am turning into a shadow of myself; I am engulfed in a conflagration I cannot extinguish and will eventually consume me altogether.'

The term for this step is becoming resolved. Resolve can be an evaluation of costs and benefits. It can even be an act of desperation in the face of losing the battle, or losing everything else of value in the process of continuing to try to win the battle: this latter is the plight of the prodigal son, who only in utter poverty realizes his all-consuming conflict with his father (and perhaps his brother) has robbed him of every relationship, possession and value in his life, culminating with his dignity. Resolve may come from less than worthy motives. It may come from something as basic as survival. What matters is not where it's coming from, but where it's going. Conflict can become like an addiction – a suit of clothes that it becomes impossible to imagine oneself outside of, and yet a pattern of behaviour and state of antagonism that sooner or later, whether of one's own or another's making, are revealed to be a prison. To escape that prison may involve reaching back to a time before things were like this, or forward to a future when they might no longer be like this, or across to lives of others that are not submerged in conflict like this. Whichever it is, it's about saying, 'This is not fundamentally who I am.'

In the words of Nelson Mandela, 'As I walked out the door toward the gate that would lead to my freedom, I knew if I didn't leave my bitterness and hatred behind, I'd still be in prison.' Mandela realized that the prison of bitterness and hatred could damage him in a way incarceration on Robben Island never would. And the only person able to dismantle the bitterness and hatred was him. As long as he continued to keep a score of wrongs that convinced him, and proved to the world, that he was more sinned against than sinning, that score would always make him a prisoner. Mandela had to let go of the fantasy that the battle against his oppressors was one he could win without turning into an oppressor himself. His example showed a whole nation that if he could be resolved to say, 'This is not fundamentally who I am', then so could everyone else.

Mandela could have dealt with conflict by relying on the sheer weight of numbers and extent of global support simply to blow the white majority away. But that would have confirmed what so many had predicted – that the transfer of power would entail a bloodbath that would devour its children and scar the nation for generations; predictions that were cited to justify the apartheid regime for so long. To find another way, Mandela had to confront not the devil without but the demons within. That process yielded resolve.

At this point it's pertinent to identify the terms that pervade this discussion. *Peace* is not a past state to which we expect, and feel entitled, to return, but is instead an aspiration towards which we ask to be led and at which we never expect fully to arrive. It's a gift, not an achievement or a right. It consists fundamentally in restored relationships, not in a personal sense of wellbeing or awareness of transcendence. It's always a work in progress.

The alternatives to peace may be divided between the apparent and the genuine. By this I mean it's important to distinguish between difference, tension, conflict and violence – all of which can operate on a personal or political level. *Difference* is created, life-giving, unavoidable and good. There's no essential reason to connect difference to conflict and violence: indeed, finding ways not to do so is integral to any path to peace. *Tension* arises when difference is experienced as problematic. This may be because an individual or group simply finds change or challenge arduous, or has underestimated the time or effort required to listen,

8

explain, understand and discover. It can be because pre-existing insecurity, anxiety, fear or envy focus on difference as a problem; or it can be because thoughtlessness or malign intent linger around the fringes of an encounter or relationship. *Conflict* is the moment when simmering tension turns into explicit confrontation. Whereas tension may sometimes be benign, even creative, conflict never is.

There are two further steps that indicate why conflict is so dangerous. *War* refers to the step where conflict has gone beyond short-term, relatively limited displays of extreme tension into a conflagration in which one or more of the parties have lost sense of boundaries or proportion. *Violence* is by no means always a feature of conflict, but is invariably a characteristic of war: it's the physical or structural attempt to dominate and subjugate the other, arising from meticulous planning or spontaneous rage.

From this list it should be clear that the *apparent* alternatives to peace are difference and some forms of tension: these are apparent but not real, for there's no reason why they can't be understood as aspects of peace. By contrast, the *genuine* alternatives to peace are malign forms of tension, plus conflict, war and violence. The path towards peace lies in highlighting, fostering and propagating the perception of difference as creative, generative and a form of blessing. The path to peace lies beyond that, in learning to harness the dynamic and life-giving aspects of tension. But this also requires us to dispel the fear, suspicion and insecurity that can permit tension to turn into conflict. The path to peace does not lie in diminishing or obscuring difference, or seeking to avoid all forms of tension. The first step on the path to peace is to recognize how enmeshed we are in conflict, and how slow we are to enter a process that leads to genuine peace; and to resolve to approach difference and tension in a better way.

2

Cease to Fight

Here's a mundane example to introduce the twelve steps. You get an email from a colleague that makes you very cross. You press 'Reply', and are all set to volley back some stinging words; but you pause, and think to yourself, 'Why am I doing this? I'm only going to get into a spat, and I still have to work with this person' (step 1). So you don't reply, even though that means leaving your colleague's ridiculous and infuriatingly sarcastic remarks unanswered (step 2). Eventually you pick up the phone and say, 'Have you got time for a coffee?' and the two of you find the courage to get to the bottom of why you're so cross with each other (step 3). You recognize you've been among a number of colleagues who've marginalized your antagonist, and you say, 'I can see how my actions have made you feel excluded. I'm sorry. It's coming from my own insecurity' (step 4). Next morning you drop off a couple of doughnuts on your colleague's desk before work (step 5). Your antagonist sends a message later: 'Thanks for the chat, and for the doughnuts. How about we try to be sure to use email for positive remarks and regular information in future, and have coffee when there's something difficult to say?' (step 6).

That's probably all there is to it. But you may find the incident stirs you to reflect on an array of fragile professional and personal relationships, and an ingrained habit to strike first, which you realize comes from your own anxiety – and you may say, 'It's time I did something about this' (step 7). You may further decide there are a good number of other 'coffees' you might do well to have with family members, friends, acquaintances and colleagues (step 8). Some of these may evoke cathartic conversations that, in time, lead to deeper disclosure, truer relationship and more honest dialogue (step 9). You might even go back to the original work colleague and say, 'You know, I'm actually glad for that spat we had and the coffees we've had since, because somehow you and it have taught me some important lessons that have ended up changing my life' (step 10). It's even possible that, seeing the change in you, a different spirit begins to pervade the office and your family and some of the places you spend time – not just in a different approach to email, but in turning tension to creative ends (step 11). And this may begin a movement that brings blessing and grace to many (step 12).

This book is by no means limited to such simple examples; on the contrary, it attempts to encompass profoundly complex, wide-ranging, long-term and troubling examples too. But if peace is about learning a different set of habits, and if peace begins with seeing the creativity, rather than the destructiveness, of tension, then the size of the problem needn't be the principal issue. Of course you may choose not to proceed with the coffee because of a significant power imbalance that makes you fear the exercise would be a charade. But at this step the point is to grasp what 'coffee' can mean. And to see why step 1, handled appropriately, may be the beginning of turning a ticklish problem into a limitless opportunity – however understandable the reluctance to engage may be.

And so to ceasefire. Imagine two pupils in full dudgeon, fists and punches flailing away. When the flustered teacher approaches and separates the battered from the assailant, it's conventional then to demand, 'What exactly is going on?' The question is apparently obtuse, because it's obvious that the two parties are in violent conflict. But it's an appropriate way to bring the respective parties to their senses, as the subsequent dialogue invariably reveals.

Broadly three answers surface.

- 'He started it' is customarily the response of the party that was winning the battle at the time of its interruption. It's a tacit acknowledgement that the degree of retaliatory violence was disproportionate, the punishment inflicted has already exceeded the hurt that occasioned the conflagration, and the balance of power is significantly and perhaps indisputably weighted in the winning party's favour.

- 'He stole my …' is the plaintive wail of the weaker party, drawn foolishly, hastily or inexorably into a conflict wherein it became immediately or eventually apparent that when violence ensued, he was going to lose, and perhaps be seriously hurt. The reference to goods stolen may be just the beginning of a litany of injustices perpetrated by this assailant or others, in response to which violence seems the only, the necessary or the unavoidable form of protest or resistance. Whereas the first response gives a story but not a reason, the second response offers violence as the necessary or inevitable outcome of direct conflict (in this case, an interrupted act of stealing). Neither offers any prospect of resolution, beyond the physical harm inflicted on the defeated party proving so great that, regardless of the justice of the case, the victor can claim complete dominance.

- By contrast, the third response, 'We were only playing', is at the same time more obfuscating and more sinister. Besides being an evident distortion of the facts, facts the teacher has plainly witnessed, it asserts that the pugilists inhabit a narrative the teacher can only partly understand. The assertion is that what's at work is not the law of the jungle, where the mightiest wins, but the law of the family, where all is part of an ongoing pattern of training, puppy love, role play, banter and kidology, where no harm is done and all happens within a penumbra of trust and security. Needless to say, it's invariably the person winning the fight that offers this account of events. But at root it's a form of denial – denial that this is, indeed, what it looks like: a violent conflict.

While it's seldom the case in all-out war, particularly of the political and social kind, a significant inhibitor to initiating a process of peace can be denial that there is any serious conflict that needs addressing. This may, as in the case of the playground tussle, be the dominant party's desire to suppress the true nature and anticipated outcome of its activity. But in more equal scenarios, it can be the deep resistance of both parties to acknowledge how profoundly invested and implicated they have each become in a situation that has long ago escalated from tension into conflict, and is close to war by all means short of violence. (Violence has to be avoided, less because of the risk of personal injury than precisely because it makes the conflict undeniable, to others and to oneself, and so often unleashes impulses that are beyond control. For these reasons it is sometimes described as 'beneath my dignity' – a telling phrase that in reality masks the urge to deny the degree to which the malign has become the normal.)

As the politician Hiram Johnson (or was it the playwright Aeschylus?) said, the first casualty of war is truth. But untruth can mean denying there's a war in the first place. Among the first steps to making peace is to say, 'We are enemies' – and to recognize the tragedy, grief and failure of that. From there it's sometimes possible to say, 'I don't believe this condition represents the best intentions of either of us.' And then, building on step 1, to say, 'This condition is bringing out the worst in us. If I don't like what it's turning me into, I can't believe you're enjoying what it's turning you into.'

What makes people enemies? Often it's a story: a story that one party has absorbed into their identity, and a story into which that party has inserted the other party as an antagonist. The story may be one in which my people have been feuding with your people for generations, ever since an affront to property, life, dignity or prosperity, and the peremptory or disproportionate revenge that followed. Frequently it's deep-lying insecurity, that there's not enough to go round or that the strong will inevitably dominate, and thus an impulse to strike first, lest one find oneself on the back foot. Sometimes it's ignorance, or a lack of information, that leads one party to impute motives to another party that assume malevolent scheming, but can, with cultural understanding, turn out to have an innocent explanation. But when all the false stories have been exposed, all the competition over scarce resources stilled, and all cultural misunderstanding addressed, there remains an ineradicable perversity in the human heart: a tendency to selfishness, cruelty, pride and greed that can trigger an argument in an empty room, and a shortness of temper and failure of communication that can turn such a conflict into violence and war.

It's simply said and apparently obvious, but constantly forgotten or underappreciated, that you can't stop a conflict until you admit that you've started one, or at least acknowledge that a conflict has started of which you're an interested party. To say, 'We are enemies' is less often the beginning of a conflict than the beginning of the end of one. It's the naming of a relationship that's at odds with other relationships – that's provisional, sub-optimal, in need of attention, the potential source of many evils. It's the start of a process of furnishing resources to transform the antagonism, rather than perpetuate it. It's a recognition that bad things don't just go away if you ignore them; that life isn't a perpetual distraction from the unpleasant; that conflict has a primal quality that infests the gut and infects the soul, and defies merely rational dismantling.

It's equally obvious, but just as often overlooked, that at the moment of cessation of active hostility, the respective parties will probably each have a deeper awareness of hurts received than wrongs inflicted, and will doubtless sincerely believe they are the innocent party, whose actions were certainly reasonable, quite possibly necessary, and in either case right and proper. The point to insist upon is that if you allow yourself to believe a ceasefire is impossible until there's an externally validated and internally perceived balance of injury and righteousness on both sides, then a ceasefire will never come. A ceasefire is never the moment when entangled parties or outside observers judge that justice has been done. It's the moment when a quiet voice says, 'Further acts of hostility will make eventual peace harder rather than easier, and drag parties that have begun to perceive an identity outside and beyond this battle back into the mire' – and when, for a moment, that quiet voice prevails.

A ceasefire doesn't necessarily mean the abandonment of hatred, the lapse of grievance, or the end of anger. Such achievements are seldom gained even by victory, let alone the suspension of acts of hostility. But it offers a platform from which to begin, a platform that renounces any more acts that perpetuate conflict, war or violence. It may be possible to go and find a 'teacher' – a third party whose intervention or interposition separates the parties and diverts attention from the object of fury. In some cases, after much heart-searching, recognition of humiliation, and honesty about the realities and prospects, there may be an instance of outright surrender. Whichever it is, it involves an appreciation that nothing else can start unless this stops.

An addict has to realize that the only way to break the addiction and begin a journey towards wholeness and wellbeing is to stop the substance consumption or compulsive behaviour that's the centre of the disorder. Something new is also required: but something old has to be renounced. Likewise, the party in the midst of violent conflict has to find a way to remove themselves, find temporary protection, call in a third agent to patrol a boundary, or otherwise withhold hostile manoeuvres, so that a new mode of interaction can emerge. It will almost inevitably feel unjust. There will invariably be a sense of unfinished business. There will be an almost irresistible impulse to demonstrate to third parties the rightness of one's cause and the wrongness and perfidy of one's antagonist. There will be an ingrained sense of moves that could have been made, attacks that could have proved definitive, opportunities that even at this late stage could have made all the difference. There may be a sense of physical danger, a fear that the terms of the ceasefire must address.

But deep down, sooner or later, particularly if this development has arisen through one party's or both parties' sense of how much they have been (or allowed themselves to be) demeaned, disfigured and deranged by this conflict, there should emerge some sense of relief. Relief that antagonism, for once, is not the stuff of every waking thought. Relief that needing to be a step ahead of the enemy need not, at last, obscure every other creative thought or life-giving emotion. Relief that the true goods of existence – love, joy, trust, togetherness, discovery, gentleness and kindness – need not, finally, be set aside for a more pressing and visceral demand. Relief that a permanent state of tension may yield, eventually, to a more relaxed rhythm of highs and lows, mundane interludes and exciting moments, in which regular existence may be resumed. Relief that one's true person may begin once again to appear from behind the mask of ferocious and combative hostility.

Ceasefire is by no means to be confused with peace. It's unquestionably insufficient; but it's equally certainly necessary. Peace names the whole journey – a journey that transcends limited notions of order. Ceasefire is one of the very first steps. It means the abandonment of myths, such as the 'war to end all wars'. It requires the jettisoning of deep impulses – 'If I had just one more day, week, month …' It entails the exposure of profound illusions – 'To right this wrong will make peace easier in the end.'

But fundamentally ceasefire necessitates a reconception of the whole notion of peace. If peace is the absence of war, ceasefire and peace are the same thing. But if peace is a long and almost never-complete process, within which ceasefire is an early, crucial, but on its own inadequate and frequently even unjust step, then they are far from being synonyms. Ceasefire is a loss undergone for a greater, yet deferred, gain. It's almost inherently unsatisfactory, because it excludes, as yet, all the other steps on which this book elaborates. It's also unsatisfactory because, perhaps alone of the first ten steps, it refers to something you stop doing, rather than something you start doing. You stop doing it because you realize that so long as you continue to do it, you can't do anything else. Nonetheless the apparently passive quality of ceasing to fight in great part explains why it feels unsatisfactory. You enter conflict, particularly violent conflict, in the assumption that you are capable of taking active steps to make things better, or at least less bad – by defending yourself and those you cherish from a threat, perhaps. A ceasefire is a recognition that such an assumption was misguided; you might indeed have mitigated the damage of an assault, but the battle has generated more trouble than it was worth, and you've become (or are becoming) a person unrecognizable to your former self. Thus a ceasefire, while often a remarkable achievement in the heat of virulent hostility, is still an admission of failure from one or more, often both, parties.

When the IRA declared the end of its military campaign, it had not given up its sense of grievance against Britain, or its dissonance with those of Unionist convictions; neither had it renounced its longing for a united Ireland. But it did accept that violence was perpetuating a conflict neither party was ever going to win, a conflict that was destroying the very culture that both sides were claiming to uphold; and was creating an echo chamber of grief that had turned a sincerely pursued cause into a never-ending spiral of bitter reprisals. A ceasefire wasn't a declaration of peace; but it was the end of a descent into purposeless war.

There's little joy in ceasefire. But the longest journey begins with a single step. And once you've resolved to live a better life, the journey to peace begins by ceasing to believe that war will get you there.

3

Tell a Truthful Story

Love keeps no score of wrongs. Hatred and enmity certainly do. Be it sectarian antagonism in the Balkans or a poisonous marriage, the nursing of resentments and the memory of victimhood can envelop almost the whole story of the past. At an early stage in the process of peace an attempt must be begun to articulate a truthful story. If that story begins with all the responsibility on one set of shoulders, it probably hasn't gone back early enough. Using the definitions outlined earlier, the story needs to go back at least as far as the surfacing of tension, whether that initially be benign, understandable or malign.

As the story takes shape, and the resentments and bitterness of each party blend in like eggs and flour into a mixing bowl, it may begin to be possible to articulate that there have been shortcomings and bad faith on both sides; or at least that one party was under pressures that stretched it to breaking point, even if the other party wasn't responsible for those pressures. Even those that unequivocally believe in the justice of their cause may be able to accept that they've not always pursued that cause in the most gracious and respectful way. Once both parties have set aside the insistence on settling the question of who started it in favour of the determination to answer the question of how to stop it, it may begin to be possible to accept mixed motives, exaggerated responses, hasty judgements, false assumptions and excessive demonization. In the words of Nelson Mandela, 'Resentment is like drinking poison and then hoping it will kill your enemies.'

At this point we must recognize the significance of power differentials. In the words of Benjamin Franklin, 'Democracy is two wolves and a lamb voting on what to have for lunch. Liberty is a well-armed lamb contesting the vote.' When all the power appears to lie with one party to a dispute, the familiar expression, 'there was wrong on both sides', may not be accurate or helpful. A 'well-armed lamb contesting the vote' is responding legitimately to a profound imbalance of power, often described as structural injustice.

For example, if there is radical inequality in land ownership, constant police harassment, predatory behaviour from corporations seizing property from peasants, and a dictatorship backed by overseas powers, then landless labourers are in a state of oppression that amounts to the regular infliction of violence. If those labourers become a 'well-armed lamb contesting the vote' by organizing mass protests or resorting to guerrilla warfare, their resistance is going to provoke a rapid and ruthless governmental reaction. Such reaction may well be assumed by observers and supported by other nations as the appropriate assertion of law and order. When 'law and order' is invoked to protect the oppressor, it's an impoverishment of law and a distortion of order. Only if outsiders have been aware of the oppression that triggered the 'well-armed lamb' to 'contest the vote' will the truth of the story become clear. It's not so much a matter of 'wrong on both sides' as one group's increasingly desperate attempts to resist the merciless predation of another.

This is not to say that any activity of an oppressed group, however murderous, militant or marauding it might be, is inherently justified because of the degree of suffering to which it is responding. What it's saying is that, until a truthful story of the circumstances of oppression have been told, until the systematic planning of that subjugation is revealed, and until the complicity of significant numbers of beneficiaries inside and outside the country has been exposed, any attempt to list the wrongs of the resistance is premature. Once the true nature of the rapacious economy and corrupt society is disclosed, other crimes and cruelties can begin to emerge, set within a context that explains, even when it doesn't justify. This is what it means to tell a truthful story by going back to where the story begins.

Such a truthful story might go like this. There was a time when indigenous peoples had vibrant, sustainable societies, with established patterns of food production, government and conflict resolution. It happened that adventurers joined with youngest sons, and others who had little stake in static societies, to seek their fortune in the New World. Their greater technology and resources meant they were often able to subjugate indigenous peoples, although they remained fearful that those peoples would regain the upper hand. So patterns of oppression became common, and it was considered acceptable to regard the dominated people as of less than human worth. Generations later, intermarriage had blurred racial distinctions, less visible gradations of class and culture pervaded society, and economic crises rendered the nations almost permanently at risk of collapse. An alliance between the military, the large landowners and the more successful industrialists justified its exploitation of the poor in the interests of security and stability, and gained ready support from foreign financiers and governments. In the absence of regular jobs with reliable terms and conditions, honest people became part of the security forces in order to create a future for themselves and their families. The situation created a powder keg where the majority of the population faced daily humiliation and degradation, and yet any form of protest only triggered greater suppression.

Such a story, though inevitably superficial in this case, begins to explain, without attempting to justify. It's a sad story. Even the greatest beneficiaries of the exploitation find themselves constantly looking over their shoulder for possible assassination, or at the prospect of eventual moves to bring them to justice, or at least some form of accountability. Meanwhile the great majority are living impoverished lives with little hope of fulfilling work, significant income, or protection from arbitrary violence or incarceration. It's a culture of fear and suspicion, in which desperate people resort to dreadful measures to survive, and honest citizens turn to adversarial actions to preserve their dignity.

When such conditions finally come to an end, and a government that more fully represents the mass of the people comes to power, that government most often finds the problems are deep-seated and the danger is of replacing one form of oppression with another. At such times there are sometimes calls for a truth and reconciliation process. These are highly appropriate, although the desire for reconciliation may too often displace or obscure the need to hear the whole of the truth. And even when the whole of the truth is heard, the fear is that truth that does not lead to justice, and reconciliation that's not derived from justice, misunderstands and bypasses indispensable parts of the process. Yet part of the truth is that the oppression was not simply constituted by individual police officers torturing individual members of the resistance, or particular government ministers accepting bribes to overlook the clearance of peasants from a particular patch of land; instead, huge imbalances of power and historic injustices create an almost unassailable legacy of distrust, corruption, fear, and flouting of the law, which takes generations to transform. Until a truthful story is told, no one can have any idea what justice might look like; until justice is done, the shape of reconciliation is hard to chart.

A point that's frequently and fervently made at this juncture is that there can be no reconciliation without justice. About this, two things may be said – a yes and a no.

The yes is that if the oppression is not to be perpetuated, if the cycle is to be broken, truth must lead to accountability. A power must arise that stops two wolves eating the lamb for lunch over and over again – an authority that represents something different from the lamb becoming sufficiently well armed to stand its ground and threaten the wolves in return. The name for this power is justice. Justice denotes the way society is organized to prevent power obscuring truth and evading accountability. At its best, justice can offer dispassionate assessment, rational evaluation, sober apportionment of responsibility, and careful conclusions. It can say, 'You did this; you did this many times; it was wrong; there's a law against it; you're accountable for what you've done and the consequences of what you've done; you will accordingly have to undergo a form of punishment that restricts your liberty and, for a period after that punishment is complete, you will continue to bear the shadow of guilt as a sign of the danger you pose to the wellbeing of others; after which period, your liberty will be fully restored.' If all the wrongs of the doleful story could be addressed in this way, a sense of closure and due process could well be reached.

The no is, not all the wrongs of any doleful story can be treated this way. Leaving aside the fact that few countries in the world inherit, can pay for and can sustain an independent and trustworthy system of this kind, and the fact that such a process would take decades after generations of oppression, there still remain two significant reasons for caution.

The first is that justice is almost always an unsatisfactory convention. When your son has been beaten to death by security forces, acting outside the law but in ways countenanced by a ruthless government, what you want is your son back – alive, healthy, with energy, positivity and zest for life undiminished. Justice can't give you that. In that sense it's an artificial construction. Even the impulse that seeks an eye for an eye can't give you what you truly want. You don't want the death of the officers involved; you want the life of your son. Anyone who tries to tell you, 'Unless you seek the death of the officers, you evidently didn't love your son', understands neither the nature of grief nor the limitations of justice. Revenge cannot restore your son; it just robs another parent of their son. Justice is a process various parties enter into precisely because they've realized that accountability is the best thing they can hope for, given that the thing they really want is unattainable. More important than punishment, let alone revenge, are knowledge, understanding and legacy.

Knowledge means that you comprehend exactly the circumstances in which your son died – whether this was a routine killing, a coercive action that went wrong, or an individual's wilful act of cruel violence. You learn whether there was anything your son or anyone else could have done to make him less vulnerable to attack, and how much he suffered as he died. You discover how common such killings were, whether the methods used in this case were usual or unusual, and how high in the chain of command such actions were sanctioned. *Understanding* means you appreciate the motivations of the killers, their bosses and the regime in general. You realize how extensively in national life and international politics this killing represented a whole ethos and strategy, in both its venal and plausible dimensions. You grasp the social situation of the security officers, their family circumstances, their similarity to and difference from you, to what extent they were proud or ashamed of what they'd done. *Legacy* means your desire that no one die a death like this again. You seek to outlaw the form of weapon used for the killing. You attempt to bring to justice not just the killers but all those who promoted a policy that made such a death normal. You build solidarity with other families of the disappeared and murdered. You try to bring some good out of such unspeakable evil.

Justice can provide a means towards knowledge, understanding and legacy. But when it does not, mere accountability is no substitute. By accountability I mean identifying who is answerable, apportioning blame, establishing liability, insisting that individuals explain their actions, passing judgement, and laying down punishment. This is a great deal: the proud achievement and fervent aspiration of any justice system. But this is not enough. What is needed most of all is the telling, hearing and establishing of a truthful story – without which knowledge, understanding and legacy are unachievable, and all the subsequent steps outlined below are hampered.

The second reason for caution in relation to justice is that justice can only work for public acts that qualify for public response. While the injustices considered in this chapter fall mostly into this category, particularly where there's a deliberate misuse of power by a dominant party towards a weaker party, injustice by no means throws a blanket over every kind of hurt, damage or grief arising from tension or conflict. There are a great many circumstances where grievance is deeply felt and cruelty or selfishness is tangible, but where the processes of justice and the wooden handle of the law can bring no solace or resolution. Yet in such cases what remains vital is the telling of a truthful story.

Let us imagine a husband waves his wife off each Tuesday and Thursday night for her regular sessions at the gym. One Tuesday he decides, as a surprise, to join her – but, to his dismay, finds neither she nor her car are at the gym. Later he asks her, 'How was the gym?' and she replies, 'Fine, like normal.' Highly suspicious, that Thursday he follows her and finds she's gone not to the gym but to a house nearby, where she's greeted with a passionate kiss at the door by a handsome stranger. On her return that evening, her husband confronts her with circumstantial evidence of her infidelity. She realizes there's little point in her denying what he has witnessed. But she quickly goes on the attack: what about the fact he's never remembered her birthday or their anniversary; what about him always going for a Friday drink with his mates, regardless of what she might want to do; how about the way he's never supported her by embracing her child from a previous relationship? The argument escalates and she ends up spending that night at her sister's house.

Justice is no help here. There may be a residual appeal to fairness – to which the wife resorts in bringing forward examples of her husband's lack of investment in their relationship. But there's no external comparative judgement on various kinds of unfaithfulness – on how many missed children's parties equate to an act of adultery. What the husband needs are answers to the following questions. How many times and in exactly what circumstances have you been with him? What lies have you told me, and for how long? What promises have you made to him? Will you undertake never to see him again – or at least to have no communication with him, and only to see him in formal settings when others are present? What exactly made you do it? Do you love me? Do you love him? Will you do everything in your power to restore trust, explain behaviour, communicate honestly, and outlast my hurt? Will you thoroughly search your soul to find out why this happened, and act differently so as to prevent situations like this ever arising again?

Only when a truthful story has been established in this way can wider questions be addressed, such as to what extent he colluded by ignoring anomalies or paying little attention to mood swings, whether his truculent behaviour was indeed a damaging alternative form of disinvestment in the marriage, and whether he himself is committed to the relationship and determined to seek in every way to make this a wake-up call rather than a torpedo beneath the waterline. These wider questions are all important and relevant, but can seldom be explored in any depth until a truthful story has been detailed about the most obvious and egregious transgression. That truthful story will no doubt incorporate many of the questions that need addressing, lies that have become habitual, and behaviours that are incompatible with restoring and sustaining trust. But to establish that truthful story will take some kind of a bargain: 'I want you to describe every single time you went to meet that man and the whole history of whether it was an exciting adventure, a way of getting at me, or a serious and sustained project of developing an alternative and eventually permanent marriage. In return I accept from the outset that there will be things I too need to name, and I promise not to interrupt your narrative with intemperate displays of hurt or anger.'

What the judicial killing and the adultery examples have in common is that feelings of grief, fury and the desire for revenge may abound and be at times all-consuming. But what the people at the eye of the storm need most of all is not justice as such, but something that justice can sometimes facilitate, and that without justice must be found in other ways: knowledge, understanding and legacy. Knowledge of what really happened; understanding of why; and legacy that it won't happen again. Those are things justice can't always give – and in some cases can never give; but a truthful story can.

Because if you are to emerge from enmity, you must transform truth from your enemy into a friend.

4

Say Sorry

What turns an emerging truthful story into a new form of action and reaction is an apology. An apology is a form of words that expresses both acknowledgement of *responsibility*, without resort to mitigating excuse, and genuine *sorrow*, not simply for the significant *hurt* and the irreplaceable *damage*, but also for the wrong *intention* that brought about such hurt and damage. In a great many cases an apology needs to be expressed by both parties. For example in a war, whatever the original cause, it's almost inevitable that atrocities will have been perpetrated by both sides. Likewise in the breakdown of a relationship, it's unusual if the blame lies entirely with one partner. But for the sake of simplicity, in this chapter I assume an injured party and an aggressor who caused the injury.

It's important to isolate the five key terms in the description above and elaborate on each one. Acknowledgement of *responsibility* means that 'I regret that you were offended' is not an apology; 'I hurt you' is. That responsibility should not be offset by excuses: step 3 allows space for a story to be told that offers context for rash, cruel and regrettable actions; here at step 4 it's time not for context or mitigation but for unambiguous admission of guilt. 'I did it': in many cases, simple as that.

It is not that excuses may not be plausible, sincere and, at a later stage in the process, part of the knowledge and understanding that make up the full and thorough account that constitutes a truthful story. The issue is timing. At this stage the immediate impulse is to deny that anything happened, or if that can't be gainsaid, to maintain that my part in what took place was negligible or non-existent, or if that can't be sustained, to assert that my actions were wholly or largely coerced or determined by others and did not and do not represent my true self or intention, then or now. So an excuse doesn't communicate a willingness to contribute amplifying detail to an agreed story: it conveys a determination to impose an alternative story. It's thus a continuation of hostilities by narrative, rather than directly combative, means. It's sometimes said that a meeting may be heated and lively in the room but it's really won or lost in the minutes. In just the same way an excuse can be a subtle or unsubtle way to win the battle once hostilities have ceased, by changing the way the events are remembered.

All parties have to take a step of trust. The aggrieved party has to trust that, by saying 'I did it', the aggressor is also saying, 'And I will make every effort to ensure I never do such a thing again' – thereby turning description to resolution. Meanwhile the aggressor has to trust that, once the aggrieved party has heard from them the vital three words, 'I did it', without mitigating excuse, there will be time and space later in the process, as knowledge is satisfied and desire for understanding grows, for wider context to be aired. What at this juncture is resisted as an unjustified attempt to shift attention from undeniable culpability to explicable error will later be welcomed as helpful background and wider perspective moving towards healthy understanding.

Expressing *sorrow* can be easily turned into a form of manipulation. The paradox is succinctly articulated in the passive-aggressive assertion, 'I *said* sorry, didn't I?' What this assertion assumes, with good grounds in culture at large, is that you can't ask for more from someone than an admission of guilt and an expression of regret. You can't hit someone, or even blame or be angry with them, if they say sorry. Sorry is the magic word that dismantles all accusation and disarms all fury. If it doesn't work the first time, simply repeat it over and over again and eventually it'll do the trick, especially if accompanied by the raising of the hand, both to identify yourself as the culprit and to ward off immediate retaliation. The trouble is, sorry, though often a very hard word to say, is just a word. It can be employed as a defence mechanism in the face of any rise in tension – a smokescreen behind which harsh words can be uttered, home truths expressed, tendentious allegations brought forward. It doesn't necessarily lead to any change, and it doesn't on its own indicate that the person fully realizes what has happened. Thus 'Sorry' is necessary but not sufficient: the sorrow must be genuine and tangible, based on a real, if not comprehensive, understanding of the harm done.

While sorry doesn't achieve a lot of things, it does accomplish some. It says, 'I was (at least in part) responsible for what happened, and I realize I will be held accountable for it.' It thus unblocks the path to the steps that follow. While the aggrieved person may very often feel the apology is inadequate, it's a vital first step; it's almost always unrealistic to expect an adequate apology until later, when the communication of greater knowledge has been matched by an appetite for genuine understanding. The expectation of knowledge (what happened) alone will seldom elicit any kind of adequate apology, because an apology will seem to make the culprit seem responsible for an unlimited sequence of wrongs, creating a combination of powerlessness and guilt that is unendurable. Thus it'll almost inevitably turn into a 'Sorry, but': 'I'm sorry for the fact your son died, but I can't be held responsible for …' In the ears of the aggrieved this is likely not to feel like a sorry at all. It won't become a real apology until genuine appetite for understanding (the why) has been shown and thus the accumulation of knowledge happens in a spirit not just of condemnation but also of comprehension – not simply or primarily to build a case for the prosecution, but more significantly to make sense of what took place without demonizing the individuals involved. Knowledge without understanding is little more than fuel for further conflagration. Only when the aggrieved person shows a perpetrator that they seriously care about the why are they likely to elicit an unambiguous apology that doesn't dribble into mitigation – a sorry but.

An apology, limited as it might almost inevitably be, also indicates that the person in question wishes things were otherwise. They're not just saying, 'I wish I hadn't been caught', or 'I wish there hadn't been unforeseen consequences of a careless or misguided act that shouldn't have had any casualties.' They're actually saying, 'I wish I hadn't acted in that way, because I now realize what came about, and I recognize that these things would not have come about had I not acted in such a way.' This is important because it shifts the moral authority towards the aggrieved party. No one is any longer saying, 'It's a dog-eat-dog world', or 'Accidents can always happen', or 'You can't always point the finger at someone just because life doesn't turn out the way you want it to.' The claims to neutrality and objectivity, accident, chance and luck have all been ruled out. We are now squarely in the territory of things that are very bad and have not happened through mischance or misadventure but instead have been explicitly brought about through a person's negligence, carelessness, selfishness or outright malice. We're able to have a conversation that's not in euphemisms and tentative attempts at even-handedness but is a genuine venture in establishing truth about real harm.

Most of all, in saying 'I did it' and 'I'm not doing it any more', let alone 'I have no intention or desire to do it again', the perpetrator is making a bridge from combat to peace that both parties can walk across. An apology is not the same as peace: but it's the beginning of peace, in the same way as ceasefire isn't peace but is at least the cessation of war. An apology has in embryo many of the steps that follow. Expecting that embryo to come to fully fledged life is premature. But elements of penance, repentance and confession are already here, and vital ingredients of forgiveness, reconciliation and healing are distantly perceptible. Apology is not to be confused with confession; it's inadequate by nature and insufficient by definition. But it breaks the logjam of 'it happened' by introducing the agency of 'I made it happen', and perhaps even 'I wanted it to happen' – and thus turns a truthful story about things that came to pass into a real story about people who brought those things about.

That harm in question is real, and of three kinds: hurt, damage and malice. *Hurt* refers to intangible, but nonetheless profound and long-lasting, effects. Perhaps the most obvious and most widespread of these is grief. It's sometimes said that almost all therapy is, in the end, about grief. It may be the loss of a loved one, as in a murder or manslaughter. But it could more generally be the loss of an imagined future, dismay at being robbed, by the discovery of lies, of a happy past as well as secure prospects, anguish at the undermining of trust that took away confidence not just in this relationship but in all others, sorrow for children who would never be born or trauma about sights that could never be unseen. Pain refers to the abiding, perhaps constant discomfort at things being profoundly wrong and terribly misshapen, leading to nightmares, sleep loss, hallucinations, flashbacks, blackouts and panic attacks. Humiliation names the public exposure and indignity of having been reduced to a condition you had never anticipated, or that no human being should ever be expected to experience. Shame is the perpetual cloud that hangs over those whom the bitter look upon with gloating, the dispossessed regard with fellow-feeling, and the respectable fear to encounter lest their loss of status prove infectious. Embracing them all is sadness, the heavy stomach and hollow eyes that know life can bring mishap and hardship, but never expected such to come from the conscious hand of one who had so little to gain from causing them ill.

Yet what is seldom immediately apparent, but may gradually come to light, is that hurt can be deep and long lasting, but may not in all cases be permanent. Beyond intangible hurt, there is tangible *damage*. Damage refers to the disfigured body, lost relative, or destroyed possessions that abide after any healing of hurt has taken place. Hurt is something that can, in some cases and often after long periods and careful processes, be healed. But damage, by definition, can't be repaired; it's gone. The arm blown off in the bomb explosion can't regrow; an artificial limb can only partly replace it: its fingers can't caress, its hand can't high-five, its elbow can't teasingly nudge. The lost relative is lost: they're not coming back; no amount of compensation or punishment can change that, and any pursuit of justice that forgets it is investing the process with hopes it cannot fulfil. The possessions destroyed in the fire cannot simply be replaced: for sure there can be new coats and shoes, sofas and staircases, but there can only ever be one child's first drawing, a couple's first Valentine card or great-grandma's handwritten recipe book. Hurt refers to suffering that can sometimes be redeemed; damage means death – the things that will never again be, which the most penitent destroyer can never restore.

The third kind of harm, in addition to hurt and damage, is *malice*. Malice refers to the malevolent will that means such hurt and damage was no accident or unfortunate collateral result but an actively sought and rigorously pursued plan. Not all harm comes about this way: negligence, carelessness and selfishness on their own may cover sufficient ground to explain why terrible things happened. But there can be a moment, or a whole disposition, in which genuine hurt and damage seems a justifiable, desirable or even essential goal. In the case of negligence or carelessness, the aggrieved party's fury is, 'Why was I or my loved one considered of such low account as to be irrelevant in the perpetrator's thoughts at the time of the incident?' In the case of selfishness, the sufferer is likely to be angry at how a person can so wilfully seek their own pleasure or security in flagrant disregard for the wellbeing of others. But in the case of actual malice, rage gives way to bewilderment that a person can become so depraved as to plot, seek and methodically execute a plan to inflict unspeakable hurt and damage on another. It's likely that, until they actually hear the perpetrator articulate such an intention in their own words, the sufferers won't quite believe it. Even with the addition of corroborating context and informed understanding, they may never comprehend how one they have so loved could, by another, be so hated. 'Everything in me wanted to kill you and I took pride in the damage I did.' This is the kind of statement that's eventually required. It's not the same as 'Sorry'. It may come a lot later. The aggrieved party may have to accept a more superficial apology for an interim period. But such a statement follows on from telling a truthful story to accept, fully and finally, that such a story wasn't just unfortunate. It was deliberate, willed and intended. And until this truth is stated, peace can't begin in earnest.

5

Make Penance

In practice an apology can go some way to address the intangible hurt and pain. But it can't make much impact on the tangible damage and loss, nor can it alone alleviate the power of the evil intention. 'It's all very well to say sorry, but ...' is the response that identifies these distinctions. A penance can show awareness of the degree of damage inflicted, by seeking to offer tangible recompense whose character is directed towards, consistent with, or at least relevant to the object in question. The point is not to aspire to full and comprehensive restitution, let alone compensatory reparation on top of that. To make such an attempt is to risk self-delusion that one can expunge one's guilt by tangible payment. Instead, the intention is to demonstrate to the victim (or the victim's survivors) that one understands the quality of what has been lost, if not fully in degree, then at least in kind. Penance is a gesture, not a due.

One way in which this can be done, corporately or interpersonally, is to identify and articulate (or visually represent) the virtues of those whose lives have been lost or inhibited, and thus manifestly demonstrate appreciation for what has been lost. It's an act of penance to write an imagined biography of a person whose life you've cut short, detailing in depth and quantity your fullest understanding of what will never be that might have been, and what a loss that is to loved ones and the world. It's an act of penance to create a memorial showing similar things. It's an act of penance to endow a scholarship to enable those from a background similar to the person you killed to flourish in their chosen path of life, whatever their financial hardship or disadvantage. It's a sombre act of penance frequently to visit the site of your wrongdoing; it's a more constructive act of penance to show what you've learned about the person you wronged, and to demonstrate how that knowledge and understanding has changed you, and thus try to create a legacy in which difference is celebrated, tension is shepherded into creativity, and conflict avoided. It's common for a nation to erect a memorial to its own soldiers' courage and sacrifice; an act of penance would be to erect a memorial or establish a programme that cherished and fostered the qualities of those who lost their lives on the other side.

This aspect of penance, in all its inadequacy, potential for good and liability to self-deception, is the subject of Ian McEwan's 2001 novel, *Atonement*, also a 2007 film. The most searing passages of the story are set in 1940 in Flanders, where Robbie, Cambridge-graduate son of a loyal country-house servant, is among the members of the British Expeditionary Force retreating to Dunkirk, having been utterly outgunned in northern France and Belgium. The scene is one of almost complete hell, the retreating soldiers harried from above by the guns and bombs of descending aircraft, and facing hunger, misery and pain from wounds, exhaustion and despair. Time after time moments of friendship, hope and energy are blasted away by relentless destruction, murderous intent and mounting odds, until finally Robbie makes his way to Dunkirk. There he finds hundreds of thousands of men who've made the same journey, thinking the hard part was done, only to find the prospects of evacuation from the colossal beach beyond imagination. All through the journey Robbie's been consoled by his last meeting with his beloved Cecilia. His utter loyalty to her and the dream of their reunion balances the companionable decency of his relationship with his fellow soldiers, and together these glimpses of the sheer goodness of love make us long for his safe return to England and to his beloved's arms. Yet as the curtain closes on this part of the story, we fear that unless he can hold his eyes open and keep sleep at bay, he could succumb to sickness or enemy fire without ever stepping on the boat home.

The novel actually begins five years earlier at a mansion in Surrey, where Robbie has returned after graduating from Cambridge University, and where he meets the highly presentable Cecilia, daughter of the household, greatly his social superior. We immediately recognize how mired in class divisions is 1930s England. But worse than that, lies and deception are everywhere. Cecilia's father is elsewhere with his mistress, her mother has retreated upstairs with a perpetual undiagnosed case of withdrawal, while numerous cousins have landed on the household so that their parents are given space to divorce as acrimoniously as possible. Robbie and Cecilia's love for each other surfaces at the very same time as Cecilia's sister Briony discovers, misunderstands and distorts it. Before the evening is over, a terrible crime has taken place, and Briony's overcharged imagination and overhasty judgement have mistakenly pinned the blame on Robbie. Robbie is led away in a police van, a sacrificial lamb doomed to pay the price for the sins of a whole household – figuratively, for a whole society. We're vividly and unambiguously shown that the Britain on the verge of war may be a place of beauty and love and creativity – but it's just as much a land of prejudice, deception, violence and the miscarriage of justice.

Cecilia, heartbroken and not permitted to visit Robbie in prison, throws herself into nursing the wounded of the Blitz and the returning wounded from the war. Briony, realizing as she grows up how wrong she was, and how profoundly she's ruined Robbie and Cecilia's lives, serves penance by renouncing her place at Cambridge to enter nursing herself. We realize that Robbie was sent to join the British Expeditionary Force as an alternative to prison; he's not a volunteer, he's a conscript prisoner. He's serving penance for a sin he never committed. We see war from many angles. We see the fragility of life, in Robbie's perilous journey to Dunkirk, in the ghastly wounds of the hospitalized soldiers, in the tenuous love Cecilia and Robbie manage to maintain. We see profound faithfulness, of the two lovers and of the various friendships that arise amid the crisis of war. And we see a kind of redemption, as each of the three main characters finds a level of dignity beyond the tawdriness of their pre-war story. Most of all we see the rapid transformation of class and hidebound tradition, as nurses in London and soldiers in France adapt to desperate situations, and the moribund class structures of the 1930s are rapidly turned upside down.

But the complexity of penance becomes explicit as the novel turns bitter and cruel. We see Briony making her penitential way to the house Cecilia and Robbie share in London, and doing her best to confess and repent of (but not explain) her false testimony that condemned Robbie to jail and the lovers to their long separation. Later we see a glorious reunion, Robbie home from the war, Cecilia at a blustery seaside cottage enveloping him in her loving arms. But then we're fast-forwarded to the 1990s, and behold Briony as a successful novelist. We grimly realize the whole account we've been given is her distorted memory of events. And we're confronted with the dreadful realization that Briony's penitent visit to the reunited couple's house, and their blissful reunion at the seaside cottage, are her fanciful attempt to save the reader from the truth. The truth is that Robbie died of septicaemia a mile from the beach at Dunkirk in 1940, while Cecilia died months later in the Blitz when the tube station in which she was sheltering from the bombing was flooded with water. There was no reunion. Briony has carried this terrible knowledge in her heart for the five decades since the war, and writing a beautiful story is her tragic way to make penance not just for her sins but for all the terrible wrongs that led to the deaths of Robbie and Cecilia and so many millions of others.

The story shows the drawbacks, perhaps the futility, of performing acts of penance when the victims of one's wrongdoing are dead and gone; but it shows the power of a person's need to shape her whole life to undertaking those actions anyway. It demonstrates how inadequate such gestures are, even when they seem the only options available besides pointless self-punishment. It exhibits, in Robbie's military service, society's recognition of the exculpatory power of penance – though the example is ironic since Robbie has committed no crime. It offers an example, in Briony's nursing career, of how a penance, when not able to address the wrong itself, can nonetheless follow an appropriate trajectory. (One could imagine a scene in which Briony might nurse a wounded Robbie, injured in the evacuation of Dunkirk.) But it also displays how elaborate attempts to atone for past wrongs, when detached from a truthful story, can devolve into fantasy and denial. In the terms of the previous two chapters, the story is one of what happens when a person tries to articulate a truthful story and jumps straight to penance without articulating any kind of apology. The result is that the penance seems arbitrary. Its arbitrariness and self-serving quality brings further hurt and damage upon Robbie and Cecilia, notwithstanding their deaths, because it undermines the power and probity of a truthful story.

A second dimension of penance, missing in Briony's account, shows its role in the transformation of the perpetrator and not just the appeasement of the victim. In this sense penance is about making a personal journey to acknowledge just how perverted one's intention was when one set out to inflict so much hurt and damage. 'I don't know what came over me' isn't enough. 'I have taken steps to understand what led me to such a course of action' is better. Penance refers to those steps. Again, they may be a gesture, rather than a full appraisal. But they're an important gesture. If I was part of a viral national movement, how was I so easily seduced? If I was trying to belong or to impress, why did I not seek a better vision? If I was obeying orders, what steps was I making to alleviate the negative effects of my actions? Trying to address such questions is a form of penance.

Briony makes no such steps in *Atonement*. At no stage does she acknowledge what the novel makes clear – that she was disgusted by (and perhaps somewhat envious of) Robbie's attraction to Cecilia, and that she projected that disgust onto the emerging story of an assault and took delight in revealing Robbie's lascivious and priapic character, as she saw it, to the wider world. Thus what others understood as an unfortunate miscarriage of justice, she came to realize was her conscious and deliberate doing. A serious form of penance would have involved not just her renouncing her academic career for a stint of nursing, but her making active and sustained attempts better to understand her unconscious drives and suppressed emotions, in order to prevent them causing further harm to others.

In the end, *Atonement* is a bitterly ironic parable about the failure of human efforts at penance to atone for sins whose consequences cannot be reversed. It's a warning to any perpetrator, lest such a person ever be tempted to think their poignant gesture or timeless tribute could ever be anywhere near sufficient to erase their crime. It provides a healthy testament to say, 'This is only step 5! Don't for a moment suppose your journey is done.' And it offers the pathos of what it means to long for what only steps 7–12 can offer, without any conviction about the source from which they come.

6

Form an Agreement

Some of the above steps are 'soft' or difficult to expose to public accountability, being personal, interpersonal or highly contextual. Step 6 is 'hard'. In some ways steps 1, 2, 4 and 5 (Become Resolved, Cease to Fight, Say Sorry, Make Penance) map much of the territory that distinguishes the articulation of an agreement from simply instigating a ceasefire. To begin to live differently, to practise habits outside the strictures and stringencies of conflict, requires confidence that the conflagration is not going to reignite at any moment, given that several trigger factors are doubtless still in play.

That confidence requires, at least, a written or similarly understood agreement about how things will be from now on. If the agreement is to work, it needs to be embedded in practices and habits that build trust and celebrate the goodness of a shared existence that transcends conflict. The agreement and the habits are equally important. An agreement without habits shrinks into a shell of formal commitment, shorn of the enfleshed substance of energy, creativity, surprise, insight and, most of all, incipient relationship. Habits without agreement rely too much on the whim of feeling, lacking the discipline of hard work that keeping a promise sometimes entails. An agreement is a contract; habits constitute a covenant: peace starts as the one and hopes to grow into the other, as it develops from grudging tolerance to emerging camaraderie.

An agreement seeks to avert the circumstances and discourage the behaviours that gave rise to the conflict. It's seldom enough to appreciate that all parties want to 'move on' or at least stop fighting; for they may be taking away very different expectations of what 'normal' might mean. And it's seldom adequate to claim, 'This will not happen again', without naming the motivations, flash-points and actions that make a recurrence almost inevitable. If peace begins at step 1 with resolve to live in a bigger story, it gains traction at step 6 with an outline of the minimum conditions of living in an alternative story.

What might these minimum conditions include? In short, realizing how far we've come in the first five steps and reinforcing the habits developed on the way. Thus in becoming resolved (step 1) we recognized we were bigger people than the impoverished beings we'd become in being so focused on winning the battle. So we need to discourage behaviours that smack of those times and develop habits that embody a different way. That means trying to avoid labels, name-calling, slurs and insults. Such terms diminish both us and our former antagonists. A glance at step 3 (Tell a Truthful Story) reveals that insults fail to tell a truthful story. Instead they perpetuate a narrative in which we are innocent victims and noble conquerors and the other group are rapacious aggressors and pathetic losers. Being bigger people means always trying to take the other party's argument at its best rather than trying to undermine the points where it's at its worst. It means eradicating the implausible parts of our story and trying to be as honest about their history as we are about ours.

Perhaps the most challenging habit, but the most vital and transformative, is to learn to see the truth as your friend, from which you have nothing to fear. This is the most remarkable fruit of telling a truthful story (step 3). Aggression is all of a piece with defensiveness, and defensiveness is often rooted precisely in suspecting that the truth does not present your cause in an entirely, or even largely, good light. But truthful speech is the foundation of trust and the bedrock of sustainable relationship: trust, truth and relationship exist and grow together in a triangle of mutual enhancement, and two out of the three can come to the rescue of the other if and when for a moment or a season it flounders. 'You always change the subject when we mention Danny' is a bold attempt to break through a wall of silence. 'Is it because you think you'll be overcome by a torrent of hatred if you start to talk about him?' is an even braver invitation to dismantle the dividing wall of hostility. 'I want you to know I'm not afraid of anything you might feel or think or say about him' clears the path for honest expression on which relationship and eventually trust can begin to grow.

A second habit, rooted in the definitions explored in becoming resolved (step 1), is to enjoy and celebrate difference, rather than being wary of it as a factor that leads to tension and thus to conflict. The way to celebrate difference is to move attention from verbs and nouns to adverbs and adjectives. Thus if you start with a verb – 'disagree' – there's an immediate threat. If you add an appropriate adverb – 'disagree well' – you are in very different territory. War is when disagreement escalates into violent conflict; peace is when disagreement is a source of vitality and energy, playfulness and humour. On its own, 'confront' is a conflict verb; the fear of tension leading to conflict may prevent a whistle-blower calling out inappropriate behaviour for a long time until it has become endemic and poisoned a whole organization (sexual harassment) or culture (racism). But when the adverb 'gently' is added to 'confront' we begin to see how an atmosphere of hostility and reprisal can be turned into an opportunity for insight, wisdom, self-knowledge, respect and, in the end, correction. Again, 'resistance' is a noun associated with subterfuge, secrecy, subversion, sabotage, espionage, concealment and underground plotting. But affix an adjective such as 'subtle', 'respectful', or even 'playful': quickly we can perceive ways to dismantle violence, disarm an antagonist and disclose a whole new dimension of discourse. There are myriad forms of resistance. Some are constructive and generative; others are conversation-stopping and likely to provoke physical retaliation.

The point is that forming an agreement doesn't mean, 'From now on we always have to agree.' You don't have to align all the verbs and nouns. What you do have to change is the adverbs and adjectives. It's not what you say, it's how you say it. It's not what you think, it's how you communicate it. It's not what you feel, it's how you act on it. In a healthy relationship, it doesn't matter what you talk about – it's the spirit in which you have the dialogue. You're no longer constantly picking a fight, looking for flaws, defending weak areas, expecting derogatory remarks, avoiding difficult subjects. Instead you're actively seeking out areas of tension, trusting that respectful, tender, kind and generous enquiry and exploration will reveal truth, enhance understanding, yield delight and turn combustible tension into creative tension. Instead of constantly and reluctantly seeking neutral territory, each getting less than they wanted, in fact settling for something a shadow of what they really wanted, in order to 'keep the peace', a healthy relationship is consistently travelling into new territory that neither party has yet colonized and where each needs the other's skills, dispositions and talents to navigate and come to belong.

In the intensity of conflict, where truth is the first casualty, every opinion becomes calcified as a fact and the facts of the other party are seen as merely opinions – or prejudices. In the habits of peace cultivated by the practices of an agreement, each opinion is tested and sorted into unfounded prejudice, debatable opinion or incontestable fact. The single practice that counts more than the others put together is listening. Again, listening requires its own set of adjectives. Not 'suspicious', 'reluctant', 'enforced', 'distracted' or 'resentful', but 'sympathetic', 'compassionate', 'curious', 'appreciative' and 'patient'. Perhaps most important of all is the silence that follows what the other person has said, however contentious, troubling or hurtful it might be. That silence says, 'I'm not going to jump straight in and refute, discredit or match what you've said, word for word.' It also says, 'Your views are your views – they may be different from mine, but I'm not shocked or threatened by them, and I don't have to take to violence to eradicate them from the earth. I can live with them as I hope in time you'll come to change some of them. If I keep some silence now I'll be able to disentangle the helpful ones from the indigestible ones.' But more than anything it says, 'Was there anything else? I suspect you haven't finished, and the more you put your anger and hurt into words, the less I fear you'll turn them into retaliation, and the more I understand what's really driving you – for I realize this conflict won't be over until we've each said everything we need to say.'

Good and thorough listening, which is the heart of telling a truthful story (step 3), is the difference between saying sorry and making penance (steps 4 and 5), being genuine and transformative and being superficial and sullen. Each party begins telling a truthful story by thinking they know what the other party is going to say. They anticipate some form of apology and penance will be expected of them, and in heart and mind they're muttering, 'Why can't we just skip telling a truthful story (step 3) and go straight to making an agreement (step 6) and move on?' But those who learn nothing from the lessons of history are condemned for ever to repeat them. Telling a truthful story is perhaps the longest step in terms of time, and the most demanding in terms of emotional commitment – in short, it invariably means changing the habits (and prejudices) of a lifetime in order to become a person who can make space for the other.

The final elements of a spirit of agreement are to be realistic and to customize arrangements to suit the parties involved. Being realistic means not being perfectionist, not running before you walk, not making the best the enemy of the good. The goal is not to eradicate difference but to make difference a source of life rather than grounds for tension and conflict. You don't have to become friends: you need to be able to respect each other. You don't have to agree: you have to learn to disagree with dignity. You needn't be too hasty in terms of expecting to forgive or becoming reconciled: you need to become wise in relation to healthy distance and appropriate dialogue. You don't always have to seek the middle ground: you can remain divided in opinion so long as you become united in finding ways to stop those divisions igniting a tinderbox.

Likewise forming an agreement isn't primarily about becoming an example to others or attracting public recognition. It's about what works for you. You might settle for something others might find appalling or offensive because you can live with it for the foreseeable future if it gets you over the line to an agreement. You might offer something others might find integral or indispensable if that's what it takes to turn ceasefire into a genuine plan for interacting differently. You might bargain and say, 'I've given way on those three things, how about you give me this one?' You're likely to need to put in question 'What we've always done' (when that's never been tested by consent), 'What's at the heart of our culture' (when the heart of your culture turns out to be inherently antagonistic to some members of that culture or to another culture), or 'What we've always been' (when resisting any change of identity was at the epicentre of the quarrel in the first place). There is no template for an agreement: it can only be hard-chiselled out of what has emerged in steps 1–5, and most of all telling a truthful story.

To take an example: addiction recovery must mean abstinence, but can't just mean abstinence. In the same way, agreement, as a complement to penance, can't just mean a dry contract. It needs new practices that turn such a contract into an active covenant. Our old antagonism has fed on malign anniversaries; when you did ghastly things to me, my people vanquished your people; I thought we were happy when all the while you were up to your neck in betraying me. So post-agreement we must create new occasions for gratitude and celebration, new memories of grace and mercy, new opportunities to affirm we're committed to see-ing ourselves and the world a different way. We must create a new language of difference that isn't about tension, a new way of saying 'I disagree' without saying 'And your view is dangerous, damaging and degraded', a new way of listening that seeks to understand rather than to gainsay or shout down.

Sometimes the power differential between those in

conflict is so great that a third party is needed to broker the agreement. An adjudicator can listen to the perspectives of each adversary and make a definitive judgement. But this judgement is about how things have been wrong in the past. It falls way short of an agreement for how things will be different in the future. Nonetheless a neutral mediator can assist in negotiating reparations that go beyond gestures of penance and can include restitution of goods and compensation for damages.

Judgement is an activity invariably conducted in an awareness of uncertainty and a sense of shame. We never know enough to be confident of the accuracy of our judgements, and this must remain humble and tentative. We can never rely on the confidence of a theorist's clear-sightedness, or on the luxury of a sceptic's withholding of judgement. Our actions may prove to be counterproductive. But we cannot not judge. Above all, forming an agreement is the moment the antagonists exchange mercy for judgement. We cannot resist judgement – often, we *must* not resist judgement. Such judgement gives us a power, because we've summed a person up in a brief way that seldom embraces the full complexity of their character and actions. That brief summary is often used to dismiss, condemn, suppress or destroy. Mercy arises at the moment a person uses the power of judgement to heal and restore, not to destroy.

7

Reach Repentance

The first six steps can stand alone. They constitute an initiative of transformation, from enmity to coexistence, offering a journey of mutual recognition and shared hope. But the rest of this book seeks to place those six steps in the context of six further steps. Those 'extra miles' that are here explored differ from the first set of six in their specific understanding of what peace means and what the twelve-step journey really is.

In theological terms, peace is Jesus. Jesus is the embodiment of God's full presence before humankind – indeed, creation – and of humankind's full presence before God. In his birth, life, death, resurrection and ascension Jesus encounters, defines and enacts what challenges peace faces, what practices peace entails, what costs peace incurs, and what prospects peace envisages. By offering a glimpse into the life of the Trinity, Jesus demonstrates the dynamic, overflowing, self-giving character of truly peaceful relationship. 'Christianity ... is the coding of transcendental difference as peace.'[2] That's to say, the difference of the persons of the Trinity from one another is the pure

---

2 John Milbank, *Theology and Social Theory: Beyond Secular Reason*, Oxford: Blackwell, 2nd edn, 2016, p. 6.

expression of diversity as harmony. Meanwhile, the
coming-into-existence of Christ as fully human and
fully divine configures the fundamental difference of
creator and creature as joyful and abundant rather
than conflictual and diminishing.

This is not a clumsy way of saying, 'You have to
be a Christian really to understand peace.' Instead
it's saying, 'Christianity is at its very heart an understanding of what peace means and a commitment to
practise that peace with friend and stranger. Christianity is modelling today the life of for ever; and peace
is another word for for ever.' As one theologian puts
it, 'Peace is the *sociality* of harmonious difference.
Violence, by contrast, is always a secondary willed
intrusion upon [the] possible infinite order (which is
actual for God).'[3]

In this context, repentance is not a heavy-handed
introduction of arcane religious terminology into a
mature and sober pursuit of sustainable life beyond
violent conflict. It's an admission that an apology,
which suggests acknowledgement of an out-of-character
misstep, is not enough: because the truth is, I am
addicted to conflict and violence. I'm captivated by a
quasi-viral force and engulfed by a malevolent spirit. I
have spurned the arts of patience, gentleness and understanding. I have seized the idea that I can destroy and
annihilate those I've come to perceive as my enemies.
The project consumes me, distorts my character and
relegates my other commitments to insignificance. As

3 Milbank, *Theology and Social Theory*, pp. 5–6. Italics
original.

long as I deny this, I remain under the power of that
force and spirit, which leads me to justify grotesque
actions and plan merciless revenge. And I'll continue to
find elaborate forms of excuse and disingenuous strategies of evasion to avoid admitting that I've shaped my
life around defeating, obliterating or at least neutering
others so that I can enjoy what I take to be the scarce
fruits of existence alone.

We may say, 'This is an absurd exaggeration', or,
'But I have very cordial relations with most neighbours,
colleagues, family members and acquaintances – this
is nonsense.' But if we return to step 1, and observe
the crucial moment when difference, having not been
enjoyed and having instead been allowed to issue as
tension, now develops not into creative tension but
into malign conflict: then we can see how our impulse
is not to travel the six steps outlined above but to be
overcome by the impulse to devolve into either passive-
aggressive resistance or actively aggressive battle: both
of which have exactly the symptoms described above.

And yes, for sure, we may choose to follow the
six steps and find a way through that conflict to sustainable coexistence underwritten by agreement. But
sooner or later we will ask ourselves, 'How much of
my life will I acquiesce in becoming consumed by conflict? How much energy will I allow myself to dissipate
in office guerrilla warfare or extended-family chronic
insurgency? How long will I be turning down a job in
a range of cities because in each of them is a person
with whom I'm not reconciled, or refusing to go for a
run in the morning for fear of encountering a person I

dread to face? How many more relationships will snap and disintegrate until I ask myself whether I'm refusing to negotiate difference more amicably? What is it in me that stubbornly puts my head down and keeps going, however destructive and depressing the recurrent outcomes?'

The choice to live differently goes back to the distinction between the two relationships made in the first sentence of this book. That choice is about choosing to embrace difference and foster creative tension, rather than seek fruitlessly to eradicate difference and ignore tension in the vain hope they will go away by themselves or be overcome by conclusive demonstrations of dominance. The moment of that choice is called repentance. Repentance is a recognition that, without God's help, one's own sustained resolution, and a supportive community, there's no hope of breaking the cycle of tension, conflict, and sometimes violence.

Repentance doesn't make much sense without step 3 – telling a truthful story. In some cases it isn't even appropriate – if, for example, that truthful story discloses that the conflict is rooted in intimidating discrepancies of power and the oppression of one party by another. A person who is the victim of an unprovoked assault does not need to repent. But most stories are not so clear cut. Even in cases where it may seem clear that one party is the aggressor, or in other forms the perpetrator or initiator, once a truthful story is told it may become easier to acknowledge that all parties have changes to make, and often fundamental reorientations to undergo. Few people are wholly innocent of a pattern of allowing tensions to become malign and thus descending into conflict. And repentance includes the commitment to take every step to ensure such a course of action never comes about again.

Repentance echoes the moment in a twelve-step recovery programme where one admits that one has lost control of one's life, that the hatred has become unmanageable, and that one has become powerless to stop the conflict on one's own. Close attention to such programmes reveals striking correspondence between recovery and repentance. Here for example are the twelve steps of Alcoholics Anonymous, first set down in the 1930s:[4]

1 We admitted we were powerless over alcohol – that our lives had become unmanageable.
2 Came to believe that a Power greater than ourselves could restore us to sanity.
3 Made a decision to turn our will and our lives over to the care of God as we understood him.
4 Made a searching and fearless moral inventory of ourselves.
5 Admitted to God, to ourselves and to another human being the exact nature of our wrongs.
6 Were entirely ready to have God remove all these defects of character.
7 Humbly asked him to remove our shortcomings.

---

4 www.alcoholics-anonymous.org.uk/about-aa/the-12-steps-of-aa.

8 Made a list of all persons we had harmed, and became willing to make amends to them all.

9 Made direct amends to such people wherever possible, except when to do so would injure them or others.

10 Continued to take personal inventory and when we were wrong promptly admitted it.

11 Sought through prayer and meditation to improve our conscious contact with God as we understood him, praying only for knowledge of his will for us and the power to carry that out.

12 Having had a spiritual awakening as the result of these steps, we tried to carry this message to alcoholics and to practice these principles in all our affairs.

I list these twelve steps to honour those who have made the connection between addiction, recovery and repentance, and to illustrate succinctly the kinds of disciplines repentance entails. In particular, this list refers to the following elements that are characteristic of what I am calling step 7.

It starts with recognition that our life is beyond our control. In so doing it makes no comparison with or judgement on other lives. It doesn't say, 'I'm not as bad as her' or 'More or less everyone does it.' It admits that our life is in the grip of something from which we cannot free ourselves. I have not become a 'bad person', but nonetheless this contagion is leading me to do many things of which I am deeply ashamed.

It then goes on to seek a partnership between myself,

God and a supportive community, by which I can discover radical change. (The twelve steps to peace recognize these three partners, but suggest that a fourth source of insight and vitality might be the former enemy, now transformed into a gift.) This involves renunciation of the will and turning that will and our life over to God; making a searching and fearless moral inventory; admitting failure; and seeking the removal of shortcomings. These are rigorous, uncompromising and daunting steps that delve deep into the heart and soul to root out the contagion, and replace it with humility, sincerity and perseverance.

Then there's the making of amends. Unlike penance, where the gestures are symbolic and indicative, here amends are direct, comprehensive and concrete forms of compensation, contrition and restitution. Whereas the agreement described in step 6 above could be an arm's-length, formal arrangement about duties, directions and compromises, this making of amends is a visceral, cathartic process of precise identification of harm, separation into hurt, damage and legacy, and a careful attempt to transform oneself rather than simply appease others.

Next there is clear-headed appreciation that there will be lapses, small and perhaps great; that these lapses will come about and potentially be expanded and elongated by the resumption of habits of self-deception; and that 'personal inventory' and immediate admission of lapse is the only way to mitigate the damaging effect of these failures. There's no sentimental assumption that repentance is a once-for-all thing, or that personal willpower can ever prove sufficient to keep a person on the right track.

Finally there is what can only be called evangelism: enthusiasm born of relishing the fruits of new existence, and the willingness and determination to turn bad to good by sharing the possibilities and methods of this new existence with all in need of it. The best way to learn is to teach; the surest way to embed these convictions in one's life is to participate in their taking salvific shape in the life of friend and stranger. This truly is, in the words of the old saying, 'One beggar telling another beggar where there's food.'

The comparison between repentance in the context of being enmeshed in conflict, and undergoing a twelve-step recovery programme in the context of addiction, yields two fruitful conclusions. One is that both require rigour, the changing of ingrained habits and behaviours, and the practice of humble, sometimes humiliating elucidation of harmful actions and encounter with those harmed by them. The other is that, while such a process is painful, it can be the secret to finding a door to glory. When an outsider sees the depth of solidarity between those in recovery, and when a stranger experiences the kinds of bonds that can grow up between former adversaries, it's not uncommon to feel a hint of envy. That envy is the unsought reward for all the struggles that bring such solidarity and companionship about. The message is not just, 'Enter recovery, because destruction and oblivion are at hand'; but 'Repent, because this is the way to true joy.'

8

Seek Mercy

To say, 'I'm sorry. I messed up', is usually helpful and constructive. But it's seldom adequate. Confession ideally includes recognition of culpability and genuine remorse. More fully than apology, it enters into an empathetic understanding of what it must be like to be in the other party's or parties' shoes, and what the story looks like if shorn of the justifying narrative that motivated the perpetrator. It's a genuine attempt to be full and final, and thus it should seek to be an exhaustive articulation of specific acts of wrongdoing. Such an account may take some time to compile, and the process of recording those discrete acts is part of the process – often a cathartic one. It comes to its climax in the seeking of mercy.

Confession would normally be a private act, for example between a penitent and a priest, or in some cases between a perpetrator and a victim, or between two or more parties to a conflict. But in some circumstances, such as a truth and reconciliation process, confession may take place in public. Again the above sequence of steps isn't comprehensive or normative, but it's seldom appropriate to expect confession of this kind early in the process. It is utterly humiliating and, like any kind of humiliation, if it's not voluntarily undertaken and offered in a context of trust, it is likely to generate bitterness that will provoke subsequent conflict.

Confession brings together steps 3, 4, 5 and 7 – the truthful story, apology, penance and repentance. But there's a reason why Roman Catholics call confession to God through a priest the sacrament of reconciliation. This name reveals how each of the previous steps has, in different ways, been about ceasing to go backwards. They are saying to a person in a hole, 'Stop digging.' Perhaps for the first time, step 8 is about coming out of the hole into the light. Confession thus continues the work repentance has begun – of making this a story not about me, but about God. Mercy is the quality that shows how confession can only fully take place in the restoration of relationship. We can witness this in a remarkable story and a scriptural parable.

The 2019 film *The Professor and the Madman*, set in London and beginning in 1872, tells the story of an American surgeon and Civil War veteran, William Chester Minor, who, in a fit of paranoid rage, and wrongly believing there to be a plot to murder him, shoots and kills one George Merrett, leaving a widow, Eliza, and six orphaned children.

The film rests on three remarkable acts of mercy. In the first, rather than be executed for his crime, William is sent to Broadmoor high-security psychiatric hospital in Berkshire, and considered criminally insane. There the warden takes a close interest in his welfare. William wins over the prison community after he uses his surgeon's skills to save the life of a badly injured prison officer. He wants to make some kind of amends for his terrible crime, and he tries to send a large sum of money to George Merrett's widow Eliza as compensation and to ease her poverty. But Eliza, in the midst of grief and fury, refuses to have anything to do with William or his money. Thus a gesture of penance (step 5) in the absence of telling a truthful story (step 3) and without an apology (step 4) proves futile and counterproductive.

But with the intervention of the warden, eventually Eliza is induced to come to Broadmoor and meet privately with William. She assumes the visit will be a one-off, and struggles to find words to express her sorrow, grief and anger. But step 3 is beginning to do its work: in due course we find a second threshold of mercy. Eliza decides to return. When she comes a third time it emerges that she can't read. William begins to teach her. In his repentance (step 7), William is discovering a life that wouldn't have been possible without the catastrophe and the new world the agreement (step 6) is opening up to both of them. Eliza brings him books. She also brings to his attention a newspaper advert placed by the compilers of the original Oxford English Dictionary.

The advert is seeking quotations from many centuries that illustrate the usage of every word in the language. William is captivated by the invitation. His exhaustive knowledge of literature, fed by Eliza's provision of books, means he sends in tens of thousands of contributions; and the work saves his sanity. But the story leaks out, and newspapers denounce the editor, James Murray, and claim the dictionary is tainted by the contributions of a murderer. And then, in a third act of mercy, James, even when threatened with losing the editorship, stands by his contributor, visits William in Broadmoor, and begins a friendship that will last the rest of his life.

The film is a study of many kinds of power. The destructive power of the gun, mental illness, public condemnation, bitterness and many kinds of imprisonment; but also the healing and transformative power of judicial leniency, restorative justice, scholarship, friendship and forgiveness.

Jesus' parable of the dishonest manager in Luke 16.1–9 doesn't come with the budget or technicolour of a Mel Gibson movie. But in just the same way it hinges on three acts of mercy, and discloses several kinds of power. The parable starts with a painful scene. It's distressing for the rich man because he's losing money; but more importantly because he's discovering that a person he trusted has taken advantage and defrauded him. It's distressing for the manager, because clearly some people in the community like him little enough to report him to his boss. When accused, the manager says nothing. He offers no defence. He doesn't give excuses; he doesn't beg for mercy; he doesn't denounce his accusers. He's obviously guilty. But here we find the first act of mercy. The rich man could have the manager thrown in jail. But he doesn't. He simply demands the manager fetch the account books, hand them over, and leave his household.

The manager calculates his options. He's not cut out for manual labour. But he's not got a deformity that would qualify him to be a beggar. So he concocts a rather more complex act of mercy. He realizes that his master's creditors won't know he's been fired, so he can continue to act as his master's manager until his master finds out what's going on. He does a deal with each of his master's creditors, by which he not only makes the creditors grateful to him but also makes them complicit with his connivance so they won't give the game away. The amounts involved are huge: 50 jugs of olive oil is a worker's wage for a year and a half. This is a second act of mercy, although a more complex and calculating one.

When the manager finally faces his day of reckoning, and hands over the account books as demanded, the rich man has limited choices. He could go to the village and tell all the creditors that their deals were invalid because the manager had already been sacked. That wouldn't do the rich man's reputation much good. So he chooses a second option: to raise an eyebrow and congratulate the manager for making a silk purse out of a sow's ear. This is the third act of mercy. The rich man would be within his rights to sell the manager and his family as slaves to recoup the debt. But he doesn't. The result is the manager succeeds not only in keeping his dignity and his freedom, but also in cultivating a great number of people so indebted to him that, even if they'd not choose to employ him, he'd always be welcome in their homes.

The parable tells us a great deal about confession, and how closely confession is tied to mercy. This is the manager's situation at the beginning of the story. He's done something really terrible, and he hasn't got a leg to stand on. He knows his guilt so deeply and the rich man knows him and the circumstances so well that he puts up no fight, makes no excuse, alleges no blame. It's a full confession. Notice the rich man doesn't pass it off as nothing. There's judgement: he's lost his job. But there's also grace: he's given time to make arrangements; and he's not punished vengefully. So in the face of full confession we see mercy doesn't mean no judgement; it means no vengeance. And no enmity.

Then the manager goes off and loses the rich man more money and takes further advantage of his generosity. This tells us that repentance and mercy don't always result in a change of heart, or gratitude, or even reconciliation. Mercy leaves the rich man vulnerable to ruthless exploitation and cynical manipulation. But the manager's knock-down deals win him friends. Even the crooked manager realizes that mercy's more profitable than a hard bargain. And then when the manager's in front of the rich man again we discover that mercy isn't always a choice. Sometimes it's the only option. But being manipulated into generosity's a whole lot better than being coerced into cruelty.

At this point it becomes clear how closely mercy is wrapped up with power. At the start the rich man uses his power over the manager not to destroy but to hold to account. Then the manager exercises his power over the creditors not to extort but to make friends. By making friends the manager has gained an unexpected power over the rich man. The rich man could destroy the manager but only at the cost of losing his own friends. But the soft power of friendships turns out to mean more to the rich man than the hard power of money and retributive justice; so he lets the manager go free. You can use power to release and to heal – or to imprison and destroy. Mercy is about using power to heal.

In *The Professor and the Madman*, mercy means using power to heal. The judge has the power to destroy William, but begins a story of healing by deeming him to be sick, not criminal, and sending him to Broadmoor Hospital instead. The widow Eliza Merrett has the power to leave William friendless, guilty and alone, but she embodies a story of reconciliation by finding grace to understand, appreciate and ultimately forgive him. James Murray, the editor, has the power to expose, humiliate and depress William by rejecting his contributions to the great dictionary, but he chooses to engage, validate and eventually befriend him instead. This is what redemption looks like: the triumph of mercy in the context of judgement.

But that leaves us wondering whether there's more to the parable of the dishonest manager than a complex tale of the power and cost of mercy. The location of this parable in the Bible is significant. It comes immediately after the parable of the prodigal son. The parable of the prodigal son isn't fundamentally about far countries or pigsties or fatted calves or parties. It's about Jesus, the one who leaves his home to reach out to the penitent younger brother and the hard-hearted elder brother alike, who prepares a banquet of mercy for all to join; which helps us see that the parable of the dishonest manager is also, fundamentally, about Jesus. It's Jesus who takes the grace of a precious window of suspended judgement; it's Jesus who goes to all and sundry not exacting the price of our debt but turning us into grateful friends; it's Jesus who goes back to the table of judgement and accepts the price of our short-comings and finally proves that mercy is the purpose of judgement. The mistake with all the parables is to try to turn them into moral tales for our ethical education. This story isn't finally about us – it's about Jesus, who welcomes us into our eternal home by discounting our failures and making us God's friends.

The film *The Professor and the Madman* isn't, in the end, about either a professor or a madman. It's about a widow against whom a terrible wrong has been done, and has been left alone to bring up six children in poverty. Yet she has the power over William's soul. She can reject his money, dismiss his apology, impoverish herself and imprison him. Or she can take the risk of encounter, trust, understanding and reconciliation. Out of that comes her rebirth, as she learns to read and devour books and enter the world they open out for her. Out of that comes William's regeneration, as he fervidly writes up thousands of examples for the dictionary. Out of that comes friendship, as William comes to meet James Murray, and an extraordinary companionship of two lonely people begins. That's what mercy does. It restores, heals and transforms, creating an ever-widening circle of grace.

Confession is so much more than a simple apology. It embraces all the seven steps that precede it, and lays itself at the judgement seat of God, humbly seeking mercy. Confession is a gamble that God's last word is not judgement but mercy. And it's a request to enter the kingdom of mercy promised by Jesus. Crucifixion is judgement. Our judgement on God, and God's judgement on us. What follows judgement, redeems judgement, defines judgement, is mercy. Mercy is the garden of joy entered through confession. Every gesture of mercy is a glimpse of resurrection.

9

Forgive

Forgiveness is a decision by one or more parties not to be defined by resentment or antagonism, to seek a bigger life than one constantly overshadowed by this painful story, and to allow one's perception of the harm received no longer to stand in highlighted isolation but to blend slowly into the myriad of wrongs and griefs to which the world has been subject across time.

Forgiveness is something that cannot be rushed, imposed, required or simulated. In some ways it is a gift bestowed by the Holy Spirit and not something a person can generate for themselves, however penitent their former adversary. But forgiveness in many cases also involves an act of will. Just as peace begins when one or more parties seek to find or rediscover an identity that's not consumed by fixation on prevailing in conflict, so at this crucial stage peace pivots on whether the injured party or parties are, in thought, emotion and will, able to let go of the uniqueness of what they have suffered and what has been done to them and allow it to join the stream of wrong that constitutes the disorder of the world.

Forgiveness is a gift when it happens not so much as a decision but as the lifting of a burden or the removal of a mask – something brought about by the Holy Spirit rather than by conscious, deliberate effort. It's not to be confused with forgetting. It's the permitting of an artist to work the slash in the painting into a yet more textured, if not more conventionally perfect, artwork than the original. Forgiveness turns the past from a storehouse of poison to a larder of nourishment; from an enemy to a friend. It is the letting-go of the longing to have a better past.

To understand forgiveness requires a careful distinction between sin and evil. Sin is living in the world as if that world were not created, sustained, redeemed and awaiting final consummation by God. More specifically it's enjoying that which should be used – making a god of ephemeral things, investing one's soul in that which is unworthy of it, in short, idolatry; or using that which should be enjoyed – instrumentalizing God, treating people as means rather than ends, wasting or destroying the good creation, in short, blasphemy. When challenged to account for our sin, we may say, bewildered, we don't know what came over us; we may respond, penitently, we have followed too much the devices and desires of our own hearts; or we may say, cynically, everyone does it, we meant no harm, no one was really hurt, others are worse than me.

What transforms sin into evil is losing what all these responses have in common – a recognition of shame, an assumption of occasional shortcoming. Evil differs on two counts: first, it is something regarded by its perpetrators not as shabby and dishonourable but positively as good and right and true; and, second, it is turned into an active programme to be implemented not just in one circumstance but in several. A sin becomes a sin against the Holy Spirit when it translates from a shameful shortcoming to a prescribed and planned rival kingdom, a full-scale alternative gospel that promises reward without grace, joy without reconciliation, triumph without mercy, gratification without compassion, vindictiveness without restraint. For such there can be no forgiveness, for forgiveness can only be a response to sin, and evil can only be reckoned with by breaking it down into individual acts of sin, which is what truth and reconciliation processes do; whereupon those acts of sin can be forgiven. Evil itself cannot be forgiven.

The Genesis 3 narrative tells how evil arises from sin – how Eve and Adam's impulse to covet the scarcity of the fruit they could not eat rendered them incapable of enjoying the abundance of the fruit they could eat. Thus they substituted resentment for grace and dwelt in a narrow domain of bitterness rather than a wide realm of glory. Sin becomes evil when this mistake is elevated to a worldview of antipathy and dictates a programme of persecution masquerading as self-defence. By saying evil arises from sin, we're avoiding any notion that evil is a primal force in the world that goes back to creation, or is any sense an equal and opposite force to good. Evil is always a secondary willed intrusion on an original grace. It should not exist; there is no logical explanation for it; it has no essence, only existence: which means that there can be no such thing as pure evil – it is always adulterated. It's a disease that plagues the world. But there was a world without it; and there will one day be such a world again.

From this account of what can be forgiven and what can't, and how the latter can be turned into the former, we can move to a second crucial distinction, that between forgiveness and love. Jesus' words 'Love your enemies' are, on the face of it, an absurd thing to say. Enemies are, practically by definition, people whom you can't love. If the command doesn't seem strange to us, perhaps we've lulled ourselves into a padded cocoon in which we've convinced ourselves we don't have enemies. In Luke 6, Jesus gives us a checklist of seven categories of enemy: those who hate you, curse you, abuse you, strike you, rob you, demand things from you and steal from you. He makes it pretty hard to say we don't have enemies.

What Jesus' words in Luke 6 show us is the difference between what it means to love and what it means to forgive. The word 'forgiveness' becomes discredited when it's used trivially – when a person has been subject to unimaginable horror and, rather than listen as they painstakingly recall each individual act of cruelty or violence or abuse, we wave them away and tell them to forgive. Even if we've had the grace to listen the person out – a process that may take years – we make a mistake if we assume forgiveness is something we can tell somebody else to do. Forgiveness comes when one is utterly fed up of being in the prison of hatred and anger and powerlessness, and reaches out for a greater story that puts the damage one has oneself suffered in the context of a great many other things that are wrong with the world. Forgiveness comes when one can't bear living any more in the story in which one is simply and only a victim – not because that story has stopped being true, but because it no longer seems like the whole truth. The reason you can't tell a friend to forgive is because if the story of hurt and pain does seem like that friend's whole story, that friend simply won't be able to hear what you are saying.

Notice in Luke 6 when Jesus gives us a list of seven ways we should behave towards our enemies, forgiveness isn't one of them. He says do good to them, bless them, pray for them, offer the other cheek, give to them, let them take from you, do not ask for restitution. But he doesn't say 'forgive'. Why not? Because he's talking about hatred, abuse and violence that's *still going on*. To forgive something that's still going on is a category mistake. Jesus offers several ways to respond and engage while the hostile and cruel and destructive actions are still going on. But forgiveness has to wait until the activity is over. You can't forgive something that's still going on, because that seems to be saying that what is going on is the whole story and therefore that it's somehow acceptable.

There are certain relationships in which trying to be nice about things and using the language of forgiveness prematurely can be a form of collusion, a way of denying what's really going on, a way of suppressing anger and deepening the cycle of despair. In some such relationships there's such a level of self-deception and compulsion and profound disorder that the hurt really is 'going on' until the day one person or the other dies.

Perhaps most prevalent among such relationships are those of intrafamilial violence. In most such contexts removing the vulnerable party or parties from such a situation is not simply justifiable – it's essential. Yet even when there is physical distance, the ingrained patterns of fear and defencelessness can run so deep that the violence is still 'going on' long after the last incidence. There is perhaps no example where the necessity of appreciating the rigour of the eight foregoing steps prior to forgiveness is more important, and where the recognition by the perpetrator of the need to complete those eight steps is so seldom found.

Another context where the inappropriate use of forgiveness is pertinent is how we think of people with whom we're at war. We defend our going to war or taking up the arms of resistance because it seems there's no other way to express our profound and utter rejection of the atrocity the other side represents, most plausibly because we've been wantonly and wilfully attacked, and we feel the urgency of defending not just ourselves and our loved ones but everything our civilization represents. And it seems meaningless to forgive people who are plotting and planning to kill, if not us, then people just like us, if not here, then in places just like here.

Jesus isn't asking us to forgive these people just now, because their hostility to us is still going on. Forgiveness may have to wait a little longer. But he *is* asking us to love these people. By recognizing that loving isn't the same as forgiving, we can give up on the anxiety that loving means condoning. Loving doesn't mean a kind of masochism that takes a perverse pleasure in being hurt and wounded. Loving doesn't mean plotting to kill me is no problem. You can't tell someone to forgive – but you can tell someone to love.

What then does loving mean, in the face of hatred and hostility? It means carefully and doggedly, not passionately or sentimentally, following the words of Jesus and the seven actions he commends to us.

1 'Do good to those who hate you.' Say by your actions, 'However much you hate me I will never hate you.' Remember this will end. Don't let these people turn you into a monster. Repay evil with good.

2 'Bless those who hate you.' Mind your speech. Try not to lose your temper. Think of those who are hating and hurting you and see them as the tiny children they once were, longing for trust and safety, and speak to them as if they were still those children.

3 'Pray for those who abuse you.' Sometimes abuse is incredibly difficult to become disentangled from. Remember God is always as much a part of any story as you are. In prayer, ask God to be made present not just to you but to your enemy.

4 'Offer the other cheek.' In other words, not just don't get into a fight, because then there'll be no difference between you and them, but don't let those who hate you think you can be intimidated by violence. Offering the other cheek means saying, 'I'm not going to accept that violence trumps everything else.'

5 'Don't withhold your shirt.' In other words, surprise

your enemy with your generosity, and thus show
your enemies you have not become like them.

6 'Give to everyone who begs.' Remember that, even
when you can only think of how you've been hurt,
there is always someone worse off than you, and
reaching out to them is a way of rescuing yourself
from self-pity.

7 'Don't ask for your property back.' Remember you
will lose everything when you die, so start living
towards your possessions in such a way that they
don't determine who you are.

When we reach the end of this list we realize that what
Jesus is describing is what is about to happen to him.
Jesus went to the cross because he loved his enemies.
As he went to the cross he was hated, cursed, abused,
struck, stripped of his clothes and humiliated. Yet at
every step he responded not with hatred but with love.
The people who did these things to him were people
like us. Only when it was almost over, when he was
nailed to the cross, did Jesus go beyond the discipline
of love and make that last step, and finally say, 'Father
forgive them. They don't know what they are doing.'
Up to that point he had loved his enemies. When it was
over he forgave them.

So when Jesus is saying, 'Love your enemies', it
means 'You have been my enemies, and I have loved
you. Don't make me into a creature of your hatred,
but let me make you into a witness of my love. Are you
going to turn into the person who hates you, or are you
going to learn what it means to love?'

This leaves two abiding questions. Can you forgive the person who makes no apology, and seeks no
mercy? And, Can you forgive yourself? They're both
questions that can be answered with the aid of the
foregoing account and the nine steps outlined thus far.
As to the first question, there's more than one kind of
forgiveness. Ideally things will follow a course more
or less as outlined in these nine steps, and the three
that follow. An enemy will want to rediscover a bigger
person than what embattlement has made them, stop
fighting, join in the lament and honesty of establishing a truthful story, make an initial apology, offer a
gesture of penance, come to an agreement, and perhaps
repent and seek mercy.

But this is not always what happens. Sometimes it's
piecemeal at best: for example in a truth and reconciliation process a person will describe in detail what took
place, but offer no word or gesture of remorse and
show no change of heart – and thus get stuck at telling a truthful story (step 3). A forgiveness that realizes
saying sorry, making penance, forming an agreement,
reaching repentance and seeking mercy (steps 4–8)
are missing can still be a genuine forgiveness, but it's
unlikely to yield being reconciled, being healed and
being raised (steps 10–12) either – and, as we've seen in
this chapter, it might better be described as love than as
forgiveness. Sometimes the enemy doesn't even get to
step 3. But the effort of will that constitutes forgiveness
– 'I am not going to let this grievous action dominate
my life, and I am not going to let hurt, fury and lust
for revenge turn me into my enemy' – though incom-

plete without restored relationship, is still valid. And in truth even if the adversary has worked conscientiously through steps 4–8, it's a vain hope that they will ever truly be able to understand how they've hurt you. Forgiving means ceasing to expect that they ever can, and refusing to let the experience of desperate harm be the defining moment of your life.

Forgiving yourself is what reaching repentance and seeking mercy (steps 7 and 8) make possible. In short, if you've recognized that this terrible act was not a casual out-of-character error but connected to a deep-seated wrong disposition in yourself; if you've made a thorough confession of not just this wrongdoing but every other that's related in any way to it; if you've taken steps to ensure no such thing ever happens again; if you've thrown yourself on the mercy of the one (or the surviving relative of the one) you've profoundly wronged, and found forgiveness in their sight; and if you've been absolved by a representative of the church – in addition to the actions of steps 1–6 – then you can do no more. But again the final step is theological. To refuse to forgive yourself is then to believe your power to ruin the story is greater than God's power to weave grace and mercy back into the story and bring good out of evil. The one abiding obstacle to forgiving yourself is then your own pride.

10

Be Reconciled

Reconciliation means seeing a future in active relationship with the one who has perpetrated so much harm; not to sustain life by keeping out of their way or erecting impenetrable fences, but to believe and discover that the former enemy holds part of the key to one's own flourishing, and that without that key one will remain in some sense still in the prison of hatred. Ideally reconciliation means turning an enemy into an ally; perhaps even a friend. It means turning difference and tension from threats into possibilities, from dangers into life forces. This is the very heart of what Christianity is about. The Christian faith is not a limited and self-serving scheme for rescuing individual souls from oblivion or worse and assigning them to everlasting life. It's the turning of the most profound energy in the universe from destruction to glory. It's imitating the way in the Trinity and in creation, difference is the secret of peace.

Conflict is many grievous things, but perhaps most simply it's a terrible waste – a waste of energy, life, time, money, talent, resources, hope. Centrally it's a waste of relationship: difference that could issue in creative partnership or rewarding companionship is perverted and turned into a pretext for destructive struggle. Reconciliation is the miracle by which the energies that have been put to malign purposes are now channelled to building understanding, forging wisdom and establishing trust. The ideal is that one day a person can say, 'You know, I could never be glad for what happened, but without it we would never have come to this better place together.'

The 1994 film *Priest* introduces us to Fr Greg, a young and rather earnest Catholic priest, new to parish ministry. The story weaves together two issues that torture and dominate his life. The first is that he's gay. Finding no legitimate outlet for this emerging part of his identity, he begins a secret relationship with a man he meets in a bar. The second is that he hears the confession of a teenage girl, Lisa. He learns that she's regularly being intimately assaulted by her father. Later the father comes to confession too, and the priest is horrified to realize that this man bears scarcely any remorse for what he is doing. The seal of the confessional means Fr Greg can't communicate this information to anyone. But he struggles with that fact just as he wrestles with his own sexual identity. The power of his ability to pronounce or withhold forgiveness feels like nothing compared to his powerlessness to stop this terrible domestic tyranny. The two traumas of his life come to a crisis at much the same time. He faces the humiliation of being arrested for behaving improperly with another man in a public place. He has the book thrown at him by his bishop, and is forced to leave the parish. Meanwhile the truth of Lisa's domestic ordeal suddenly comes to light. In a harrowing scene, Lisa's mother emerges from an angry crowd, and squaring up to Fr Greg, with a tearful, bitter and unforgiving gaze, says to him, 'You knew.' Fr Greg has no idea what to say. Lisa's mother, now in disbelief and with her fury momentarily diverted from her husband and focused on her fragile and despised priest, says, vengefully, 'You *knew*.'

The end of the film *Priest* contains a remarkable scene. Fr Greg returns to the parish after his time of humiliation and exile. The anger and hatred still smoulders in the neighbourhood and the parish. Lisa's mother's incandescent words, '*You knew*', are still ringing in his and our ears. Lisa hasn't been seen in the church since the truth about her household came to light. The senior priest, Fr Matthew, implores the congregation to receive him back as their father in God. When it comes to receiving communion, there are two stations for taking the bread, one from Fr Matthew, the other from Fr Greg. Every single worshipper at the service lines up to receive from Fr Matthew. Fr Greg stands alone, the body of Christ in his hands, totally shunned and visibly humiliated by the whole congregation. Seconds tick by; his isolation is crucifying. Somehow he has the courage and defiance to continue to stand alone. And then slowly but purposefully one solitary figure shuffles forward and stands before him to receive communion. It's Lisa.

Their eyes meet as she receives the communion bread. Her eyes say, 'I know that you knew about my dad. But I know that you couldn't do anything about it. I understand your present powerlessness. I know it's because you believe in a greater power. You show me that by your courage in being present here right now. You're being crucified, but you're showing us a love that hangs on, that will not let us go.'

This is a story of reconciliation. It's made satisfying because it's not clear that Fr Greg has done something wrong in entering a same-sex relationship, despite the Roman Catholic Church's insistence on the celibacy of the priesthood, and discouragement towards same-sex relationships in general. Neither is it clear whether he's done something wrong by keeping the seal of the confessional in the face of what Lisa's father has told him. What is clear is that the church hierarchy and the congregation disapprove of the former, and Lisa's mother and the congregation are furious about the latter. Yet Lisa, the unambiguous victim in the story, makes a decision and publicly demonstrates that she seeks a future in active relationship with Fr Greg, whatever else anyone might think, and by receiving communion from him makes clear that she accepts, indeed welcomes, him not just as a man but as her priest. The whole film is a proclamation that the grace of God can work despite the fitful understanding, clumsy rules and flawed actions of human beings and institutions, and that it works most characteristically through 'the least of these' – in this case, the most vulnerable and sinned against person of all.

Lisa receives Fr Greg back as her priest. She chooses not to blame him for upholding the seal of the confessional. She exercises such little power as she has to affirm Fr Greg. He is not her enemy; and never has been. But Lisa makes no such gesture towards her father. To do so would be another matter entirely. There can be a tendency for those with power and privilege to praise precipitate forgiveness when offered by a victim to a perpetrator. For example in the context of a repeated pattern of lethal violence pursued by security forces towards minority groups, it can happen that the sibling of a murder victim almost immediately forgives his brother's killer. But as the earlier chapters have made clear, an act of forgiveness or reconciliation without the foregoing steps – ceasefire, telling a truthful story of harm done, repentance, seeking mercy – is problematic, however sincerely intended. Yet many are quick to applaud. Their praise could be interpreted as a further layer of oppression. A different telling of the story might portray the act of forgiveness as an unwitting form of collusion. In such a case praise may be part of a denial of the persecution that is really going on.

There's more to reconciliation than making the best of a bad job. It's about returning to the two kinds of relationship at the very start of this book and realizing that seeking to live life as a refuge from conflict, by denying, avoiding or rapidly closing conflict down, isn't so much living a privileged, cossetted life, as not really living at all. That's because conflict is a terrible waste of all the good things difference and tension can yield. To try to live in denial of difference and suppression of tension is not just to store up problems for later, but to miss out on the limitless energy difference and tension can generate. The release of this energy is the adrenaline rush that comes in reconciliation. When those involved in restorative justice say they can't imagine doing anything else, they're indicating that nothing compares to the power of truth-telling, repentance, seeking mercy, forgiveness and reconciliation.

This energy corresponds to the African notion of *ubuntu*. This has been defined as 'a form of relational spirituality that connotes the basic connectedness of all human beings' – a conviction that 'My humanity is caught up, is inextricably bound up, in yours. We belong in a bundle of life ... What dehumanizes you inexorably dehumanizes me.'[5] This spirituality looks to the interconnectedness of the persons of the Trinity as a model of mutual indwelling, and seeks to imitate that respectful interdependence and coinherent identity in human relations. It also, in characteristically African manner, believes the spirits of the dead and of generations yet to come are parts of that coinherence. So by reincorporating the story of the terrible crimes and wrongs that severed a relationship, the people reconciled harness the energy of that dynamic unity-in-diversity that the Trinity embodies.

At the Last Supper, such a body disintegrated. Jesus held up a loaf of bread, and said, 'This is my body, broken for you.' It was an expression with many layers of meaning. Within minutes, the tight-knit body of disciples would be broken, as Judas left the meal to

---

5 Michael Battle, 'A Theology of Community: The Ubuntu Theology of Desmond Tutu', *Interpretation: A Journal of Bible and Theology* 54/2, April 2000, pp. 173–82 at 178, and Desmond Tutu, *No Future Without Forgiveness*, New York: Image, 2000), p. 10.

betray him to the authorities. Within hours, that body would be further broken, as Peter denied and the rest of the disciples fled. Next, Jesus' body would itself be broken, whipped by soldiers, hung out to dry, pierced by nails and a sword. But that was not all Jesus said as he held out the broken bread. He added, 'Do this and re-member me.' Break bread and re-member. A community, a friendship, a human body can be utterly broken. But it can be re-membered in God. That's Jesus' promise at the Last Supper: God will put all our members back together, and literally re-member us. That's what resurrection is. Reconciliation is an icon of resurrection.

So if we dismiss or lose patience with reconciliation, we're turning our backs on the most tangible experience of resurrection this life offers. Yet still we become exasperated with reconciliation. Either we believe a good and wholesome life should be one in which there's no struggle, and thus dismiss, deny or suppress conflict, or we tire of how lengthy and demanding reconciliation turns out to be, and hasten gratefully to a more achievable project. What we meanwhile invariably fail to appreciate is that this more amenable project is no more and no less than an apparently more attainable form of reconciliation. Reconciliation *is* the human project – with God, one another, ourselves and the earth. All activity is some form of reconciliation – some part of the twelve-step agenda, some way of restoring what has been broken. There's no alternative to reconciliation. Reconciliation is the gospel. It's also the whole life of God. There's nothing in God that's not constantly about the work of reconciliation, with us and with creation. God has no other, more pressing or attractive thing to do than meet face to face with members of the human race that betrayed, denied and killed God's beloved – and continue to do so.

The paradox of reconciliation is that both parties cannot be glad at the ghastly events that have taken place and that at least one of them has perpetrated; but they nonetheless would not have wished to live without the relationship that would never have come about had those events not happened.

When a deranged attacker has assaulted and killed a close member of your family, you will be devastated, bereft, bewildered – lost in grief, then longing to know what happened, why it took place, how the culprit can be brought to justice, and how such things can become less common in future. But the evidence that emerges at the trial, and such justice as comes about there, are not the end of the story. The truth is, the perpetrator of this crime will always be in the room, will constantly be practically a member of your family, whenever the family gets together, whenever the phone rings and it isn't your loved one calling, whenever you reflect on the painful past or plan for a very different future. To forgive such a person in such circumstances is to attempt to diminish their power over you, to dismantle the mystery and horror and turn them into sadness and acceptance. But forgiveness, especially in the absence of the perpetrator carrying out steps 4–8 as described in this book, is still not enough to take away the power of this event to overshadow and dominate your life.

If this person is de facto a member of your family, because they are always in the room, you may need them indeed to be in the room. You may need them in some positive sense to *be* a member of your family, so that you find a way to narrate positively a story that will otherwise continue to poison you.

In such a case, as is common in the world of restorative justice, it's quite common for the attacker to show no awareness or remorse, and to see little need to atone for their crimes, let alone make amends and develop relationship with the victim's family. It's usual for a person who has committed many crimes to say, 'Those crimes are me: what I've done is who I am. Take the crimes away and I have no identity.' This is where telling a truthful story (step 3) can become a route into being reconciled (step 10). Introduce a truthful story, which encompasses not only the attacker's perspective and motivations, the judge and jury's perception and verdict, but now also the thick description of the quality of the life that was taken, the daily, hourly anguish of the victim's family and close friends, the misery, torment and harrowing grief, the devastated hopes and smashed dreams, the nightmares, depression and despair that have followed – all communicated, not in anger but in calm tones and sombre voice: and then very likely the mood will change, and emotions will flow, and culpability will be acknowledged, and deep sorrow, perhaps in the form described above as steps 7 and 8, will ensue. A person who has done many crimes has likely become largely impervious to anger and condemnation; what bites and digs is composed, controlled narrative, where the listener can draw their own conclusions.

At this point it's very hard for either party simply to walk away. The perpetrator, on discovering the 'real' crime, rather than simply the one attached to the events by judge and jury, will no doubt long to hear words of forgiveness – which, as I trust my outline of the several steps has shown, may be seriously premature. But the victim's family members, now that they've reached a place of genuine understanding, and broken through to a place of truth after perhaps years of bewilderment and incomprehension, are unlikely to want to draw a line. The paradox is that no one is placed to understand and share the dominant fact of their lives better than the one who brought that fact about, and now finally emerges from the fog of denial, evasion and self-deception to call it what it is. The family and the offender are locked together, like it or not. Reconciliation names the extraordinary and sometimes counterintuitive journey by which both parties come to like it.

That's what it means to love mercy.

11

Be Healed

The last two steps are gifts of the Holy Spirit rather than results of human endeavour or will. Genuine healing means finding oneself in a place where one can say, 'I am a wiser, deeper, better person than I would have been had all this not have happened. I still bear the scars, but, like Jesus' scars on Easter Day, those wounds are an indication of glory, a sign of love and an emblem of peace.' Healing is not about reversing the hurt or damage, dismantling the pain or eradicating the loss; it's about realizing one's life is no longer dominated by enmity, discovering wisdom and relationship that would not otherwise have been so, and perceiving in this benighted period a source of compassion, dignity and hope. This is more than resilience. It's the restoration of the broken and despoiled as a gift.

Few resolutions of conflict reach such a step. But this is an account of peace, rather than of the cessation of conflict. Peace is a much richer notion that simply the absence of war. Part of its mystery is its capacity to take the malign elements that go into fuelling war and transform them into the ingredients of mutual flourishing. That process is called healing.

The healing stories in the Gospels are accounts of miracles. But these miracles are not simply displays of power. They're illustrative and provocative images – parables of the way God heals the world in Jesus. Take the story in Mark 2 of the four men who break through the roof and deliver a paralysed man to Jesus, who asks, 'Which is easier – to heal him or forgive him?' before sending the man on his way, carrying his mat. The paralysed man in this story represents Israel. Israel's story is shaped by two themes. One is Exodus. Israel was in bondage, in slavery: and God set Israel free. The other is Exile. Israel was lost in Babylon. God met Israel in the place of despair and brought Israel home. The difference between the two is that Egypt was the trouble Israel got into through no fault of its own. Its liberation we can call healing. Babylon, by contrast, was trouble Israel got into through its own weakness, perversity and folly. Its liberation we can call forgiveness. At the time of Jesus, Israel was in another crisis: it was under the thumb of the Roman Empire.

So when Jesus looks at the paralysed man, he's looking at the paralysed people of Israel. And he's saying, 'Which is it? Is this like Egypt, a straitjacket you were put in by others? Or is it like Babylon, a prison you made for yourself?' To put it another way, 'What have you come to me looking for – healing or forgiveness? Which is easier, to say you're forgiven, or to say you're healed?' Those who enter what I'm calling a twelve-step process of peace have to face the same question. They start where the man in the story starts: they're paralysed. The thing they're not always sure about is, which is it? Are we paralysed because of the hurt and damage done to us by others – or the prison in which we've put ourselves? Here's forgiveness; and here's healing. Which is easier? It's not always an easy question to answer.

In the story, the four stretcher-bearers see there's a formidable barrier between Jesus and the one he's come to save, the paralysed man, or Israel as we've already called him. It takes four people to carry the paralysed man. In other words four people were bent out of shape in order to get one person into shape. It begs the question of how many people our own paralysis, our own refusal to be reconciled, bends out of shape: four people – or a whole host more? The stretcher-bearers break through the barrier from the top down. The scene enacts and playfully recasts the whole gospel story – the entirety of what Jesus is doing: breaking through the barrier between God and humanity, opening up the ceiling, coming down through the roof and coming to dwell among us. These four figures imitate what Jesus is all about. The story ends with the once-paralysed man now carrying his own stretcher – ready to carry someone else in their paralysis. Right at the beginning of his Gospel, Mark gives us a picture of resurrection. Jesus transforms this man and every one of his relationships.

Turning to two further healing stories, from Mark 7.24–37, we see again what healing entails, and where it's most needed. In Greek, healing and salvation are the same word. These three stories are showing that Jesus is bringing salvation to the Gentiles. Jesus does some terrible things in these stories. He fraternizes closely with Gentiles. He gets very close to a woman, apparently letting her touch his feet, generally associated with sexual intimacy. He spits on another human being, a taboo in almost every culture. Those are the things that would have shocked the disciples at the time. But there are two things that shock us even more. He refers to the Syrophoenician woman and her race as dogs. If you think of the racially toxic words we shun today, you can insert any one of them in here. Dogs were not cutesy pets in first-century Lebanon. They were considered disgusting. It's profoundly disturbing to hear Jesus say such a thing – not so much the expletive value, but the offensiveness of the sentiment. But then there's something even more bewildering. He changes his mind. How can God have a change of mind?

The story here comes right up against one of the most unresolved issues of our time, and a subject that has scarred church and society for centuries. It's what happens when one group of people, most influentially those who like to think of themselves as white, identify what they take to be a demarcating characteristic and make that a reason to assert their superiority over another people, justifying discriminatory policies and physical attacks upon them. The African American journalist Ta-Nehisi Coates characterizes racism as 'the need to ascribe bone-deep features to people and then humiliate, reduce, and destroy them'.[6] He insists

6 Ta-Nehisi Coates, *Between the World and Me*, New York: Spiegel & Grau, 2015, p. 8.

that 'race is the child of racism, not the father'. Difference has long been there – but difference isn't the issue; the issue is to regard physical differences as disclosing indelible marks of character and then basing a social hierarchy on those imagined marks of character. Coates sees the fundamental fault line in American society not between the rich and the poor, but between those who call themselves white and those whom they choose to call black. 'Whites' have in different ways asserted their right to dominate, humiliate and exploit the bodies of black people to maintain their own meaning, and to ensure there's always someone down in the valley, 'because a mountain is not a mountain if there is nothing below'.[7]

Speaking to his teenage son, Coates explains, 'You have been cast into a race in which the wind is always at your face and the hounds are always at your heels.'[8] He describes what coming of age means for a black person in contemporary America. He tells his son, 'What divided me from the world was not anything intrinsic to us but the actual injury done by people intent on naming us, intent on believing that what they have named us matters more than anything we could actually do. In America, the injury is not in being born with darker skin, with fuller lips, with a broader nose, but in everything that happens after.'[9] And this distinction affects almost everything in society. The most poignant example is 9/11, which Coates witnessed,

7 Coates, *Between the World and Me*, p. 105.
8 Coates, *Between the World and Me*, p. 107.
9 Coates, *Between the World and Me*, p. 120.

living in New York at the time. He admits, 'Looking out upon the ruins of America, my heart was cold.' And then he explains why: 'I kept thinking about how southern Manhattan had always been Ground Zero for us. They auctioned our bodies down there, in that same devastated, and rightly named, financial district. And there was once a burial ground for the auctioned there ... Bin Laden was not the first man to bring terror to that section of the city.'[10]

Coates dismantles two myths that the people who want to call themselves white hold dear. One is about the police. Whites maintain that police persecuting black people, and the courts sending so many black people to jail, are perversions of the law enforcement and criminal justice system. But Coates points out that such policies haven't been imposed by a repressive minority. They represent the majority view of the people who want to call themselves white. Rogue police are not an out-of-control minority; they are simply enacting what most Americans think.[11] The other myth is the mantra invariably proclaimed by whites who propagate the tradition that black bodies are of lesser value: 'I am not a racist.' Coates describes such people as 'obsessed with the politics of exoneration'. He observes wryly, 'There are no racists in America, or at least none that the people who need to be white know personally.'[12] Such people have convinced themselves

---

10 Coates, *Between the World and Me*, pp. 86–87.
11 Coates, *Between the World and Me*, pp. 78–9.
12 Coates, *Between the World and Me*, p. 97.

that their prejudice is either good, or at least conforms to some kind of natural law.

The significance of Coates' critique may not be fully grasped until we review how the Syrophoenician story is conventionally read in white circles. White readers tend to assume they are Jesus' disciples, who plausibly suppose that Jesus and the gospel are just for them. Jesus' words about the dogs seem harsh – but it seldom occurs to white readers that they themselves are the dogs. White Christians struggle to grasp that they are the outsiders like the Syrophoenician woman and the deaf man who had an impediment in his speech. The passage makes no sense unless its readers already know or are willing to find out what it means to be on the receiving end of racism.

The first story, about the Syrophoenician woman, is about race and exclusion as a collective phenomenon. God is among us; but there are many barriers between us and God, represented in the story by Jesus seeking to remain incognito. Gender and convention exacerbate those barriers. But our desperate need, and our awareness of being in the grip of malign forces, impel us to seek help. God's grace has hitherto been limited to the chosen people, the children of Israel. But in our need we are willing to accept even the crumbs that fall from the children's table. A crumb that comes from the source of true healing and redemption is far more precious than a banquet that comes from anywhere else. It's an equation that says God's mercy plus our humility equals glory.

The second story plays out the personal implications

of this seismic shift in the circumference of grace. Here is the condition of being a Gentile embodied in one person: he can't hear revelation and he struggles to articulate truth. But somehow he comes to Jesus. Jesus forms a relationship just with him, taking him aside. Jesus touches him, in a remarkably intimate way, sharing the water of life. And Jesus speaks to him. The healing represents his salvation. And straightaway the man is released into his destiny: he joins the chorus of God's praise made known in Christ.

The central phrase is the Aramaic *Ephphatha*, 'Be opened.' Everything is being opened. The man's ears, obviously, and in a sense his mouth. But also the covenant between God and Israel. And also, perhaps most fundamentally, the heart of God. What we have is a visual and tangible portrayal of the opening of God's heart towards the Gentiles – towards those who seemed inferior, excluded, unclean; to be, to use Coates' vivid language, the valleys without whose lowliness others wouldn't be confident they were mountains. The first story portrays God being opened to us. The second story portrays us being opened to God. These aren't really stories about disability or suffering: they're about salvation, and how it becomes limitlessly deep and limitlessly broad. And it is on this being-opened, this precise moment in the gospel, that the salvation of the Gentiles, deep and broad, depends. But white Christians can only appreciate it if they're prepared to walk in the shoes of a person like Ta-Nehisi Coates. This is what it means to say African Americans have an understanding of salvation that few people who need to call themselves white can fully share. It demonstrates what the Gospels proclaim but is hidden when the Bible's social character is suppressed: that healing is just as much about overcoming ostracism and bringing reconciliation after great social wrongs as it is about a personal sense of wholeness or closure.

This story also takes us back to becoming resolved (step 1) and shows how the beginning of the journey of peace is already about healing. Jesus leaves the right hand of the Father, comes down among us, reaches out to us in our exclusion and waywardness, looks us in the eye, as a people and as one person, and says, 'Be opened.' Be opened: enter into your true identity, as one who sees and praises God. You're a bigger person than your deeds as an oppressor or your condition as an oppressed person have made you. It's time to begin a change of identity.

Healing, unlike the ten steps that precede it, is an act of God. But I've explored its social dimensions, and done so through examining healing stories in the Gospels, to demonstrate that healing isn't a private, comforting, form of personal therapy. It's as powerful and essential as the foregoing ten steps. It's not a pleasant afterthought, like a happy domestic scene that conventionally concludes a TV sit-com. It's integral to the whole process of peace. Because peace is a profoundly transformative process, on every conceivable personal and public level.

12

Be Raised

Resurrection is, finally, the goal of salvation, and the end of a peace process. And in naming the goal of salvation and step 12 of this process as resurrection, we realize that salvation and a peace process are ultimately the same thing. Salvation is a peace process. A peace process is the seeking of salvation. Our engagement in a peace process and God's saving resurrection of Jesus are different in degree but not in kind. Engaging in the process of peace is the fundamental way we imitate the saving work of God in Christ, and allow ourselves to be made part of the way God is redeeming the world. It's not that we know what resurrection looks like and peace is a helpful analogy of that resurrection. The resurrection of Jesus – in its immediate sense of the body raised after crucifixion, and in its wider sense of the forgiveness, resurrection and healing that are recorded in the post-resurrection gospel accounts – is precisely an account of what peace entails. Peace is, in the end, resurrection.

But peace is only possible because of resurrection. How would anyone have the courage and temerity to begin on such an arduous and agonizing journey if they weren't confident that they were imitating the grain of the universe – the way things fundamentally, eternally are? The resurrection promises that peace will, eventually, prevail. It is better to fail in a cause that will finally succeed than to succeed in a cause that will finally fail. If resurrection, peace, is how things fundamentally, eternally are, then a faltering effort to make one's way through these twelve steps is more valuable than a flourishing attempt at any other project.

If step 12 is resurrection, and steps 10 and 11 are the first signs of that resurrection, it becomes easier to see how the previous nine steps are in different ways encounters with crucifixion. Ceasefire is an experience of how much remains unresolved, how raw injury still is, how hopeless it is to imagine reaching justice let alone healing from here. A truthful story exposes horror and agony – an insight into the suffering of the cross. Apology and penance, while valid and often indispensable steps on the journey, are wholly inadequate and point to the need for something the antagonists can't provide. An agreement may be little more than an armistice unless something fundamentally changes. Repentance is a kind of crucifixion. It involves the anguish of being divested of harmful habits and formerly ingrained assumptions. It's also the recognition that one can't do this in one's own strength: the real death is handing over control of your life to the one who really knows what's best for you. Seeking mercy and confessing sin mean finally recognizing the depth of what you've done and looking to God to narrate a different story; this is the point at which one realizes that the cross wasn't a faraway tragedy brought about by people very different from oneself, but a consequence of actions identical to one's own. Forgiveness is best understood as the work of the cross, painfully and painstakingly chiselling away our clinging to bitterness and resentment, rather than yet the true work of resurrection. Forgiveness is fundamentally a gift rather than an achievement, an allowing-to-be rather than a making-good, a recognition that we can never still the storm ourselves; all we can do is steer the ship somewhere near the harbour, and invite the pilot to take over from there.

The work of resurrection begins in earnest at step 10, when what had scarred the story as thorns begins to show its face as roses. If the first nine steps have fully yoked the process to the cross, the last three steps can truly enjoy the breathtaking possibility of resurrection. Reconciliation and healing are the closest analogies to resurrection; but are only fully understood when their family resemblances reveal them to be resurrection's forbears. More than any of the previous steps, resurrection is something we cannot achieve – only something that can happen to us. But that's no reason not to imitate its pattern with every opportunity that comes our way. And the most fertile opportunities are the ones that have slowly, painfully emerged from our experience of the previous twelve steps.

The Bible converges, for Christians, on the death and resurrection of Jesus. But once this house style is recognized, it can be discerned as anticipation or echo in many other places throughout the Scriptures. Advertisers tell us that the two most evocative words in the English language, each of which in a few letters conjures up a narrative, paints a vision, stirs the soul and loves the heart, are 'new' and 'again'. But these two words tell different stories. 'New' promises to leave behind the shabby, clumsy, broken, embarrassing, dull, feeble – in short, the old. New is all about beginning, possibility, freshness, birth. By contrast 'again' is about return, restoration, rhythm, revisiting, bringing back to life. It's about a second chance, about renewal, regeneration, an opportunity to see the familiar and the tarnished in a deeper, richer way. It's about coming home. 'New' is the word Christians use for creation. It has excitement, wonder, creativity, delight, discovery, mystery. 'Again' is the word we use for salvation. It has relief, forgiveness, tears, joy, reconciliation, trust, wisdom, mercy. 'New' is about birth; 'again' is about new birth – resurrection.

The word for the place where 'new' and 'again' meet is 'Jesus'. Jesus is Israel again, the replaying of Israel's story with God, except with a different ending this time, the chance to set right all that was wrong, to unravel injustice, restore trust and breathe life into dry bones. But Jesus is also creation made new, a new beginning, the birth of what was always meant to be, a transformation of what's possible. When people come to faith it's sometimes about discovering the new, and it's sometimes more about restoring the old, about finding faith again.

The prophet Isaiah harnesses the power of these two words, 'new' and 'again'. In the later chapters of his book, Isaiah is writing after Judah's return from exile in Babylon in the sixth century BC. Isaiah portrays the new society made possible after this amazing change in fortunes. How much will be genuinely new, and how much will be the restoration and resurrection of what was there before the 50 years of exile? It's the same question participants in a peace process are asking, as they ask God to restore the years the swarming locusts have eaten. Isaiah 58.12 anticipates how people in days to come will remember this generation: 'Your ancient ruins shall be rebuilt; you shall raise up the foundations of many generations; you shall be called the repairer of the breach, the restorer of streets to live in.' Isaiah is saying, 'You will be remembered because you looked devastation and failure and ruin squarely in the face and piece by piece you restored the ligaments, the muscles, the joints, the membranes that hold society together. You didn't build, and achieve, and create: this isn't about new; this is about again. New is good, exciting, exhilarating; but again is harder, more hidden, more subtle, more challenging.'

The phrase that describes becoming an agent of resurrection is 'the repairer of the breach'. The phrase has philosophical and practical dimensions. Philosophically, life is much more about repairing than making. The Coliseum, the great stadium in ancient Rome, has a dilapidated appearance, which may look like a symbol of the fall of a once-glorious empire. In fact most of the stones were taken away to make other buildings in the city. That's how most things are created: they're made out of the remnants of previous things. When we make a new friendship, it feels new, but in fact much of what we're bringing to it is our experience of previous friendships, both good memories and bad ones. When we make a dress, it looks new, but in fact it's made up of remnants of other things. Whenever we throw something away it goes back into the earth, and sooner or later will reappear as a raw material for something we want to call new. Likewise with professions. Physicians don't make things: they repair people. Lawyers don't make things; they mostly step in when things have gone wrong. Engineers make things: but most of the things they make are joining together two things that have got separated. They all spend their time repairing the breach.

'Repairer of the breach' is such a resonant way of talking about our calling as human beings that Jews use it as a description of what it means to be a Jew in the world today. The phrase *tikkun olam* means exactly that. It can be a breach between nations or populations, or between peoples and the planet; or a breach between parts of an organization or family; or between a person and God; or between ourselves and someone we find it hard to love.

This reveals that just as peace is resurrection, just as all work for good is a kind of peace process, so a peace process is a form of education. Education is also a kind of twelve-step programme. There was a time when education was about identifying people of talent and lifting them out of their home environments and getting them up, out and away into the fresh air of knowledge and discovery, and quite possibly making it impossible for them ever to go back. But the most important education is that which equips us to repair the breach, to be agents of community that are able to be present, restore relationships, encourage, inspire, empower, reconcile, and bring to bear all the positive resonances of the word 'again'. The greatest achievement of educators is that they become known for raising up people who are called 'repairers of the breach'.

A curriculum for making people equipped to repair the breach would need to foster suitable qualities and skills and disciplines. The place to start is to follow Isaiah's lead and wean ourselves off the notion that breaches can simply be 'fixed'. A suffering society or a dysfunctional family is a diseased body that needs healing, not a broken gadget that needs fixing. A repairing curriculum is based on learning what it means to heal – to forgive, to be reconciled, to repent, to befriend, to forge a shared story together. It's not in the business of finding a target to blame, of cutting out a cancerous person and ostracizing them, of scapegoating, labelling, ejecting and rejecting; it's about working together on issues and discovering complementary gifts.

Next on the syllabus is what it means to build networks of trust. In a conventional school, once you've shared a classroom, played on a team, sung in a choir, been on a trip, you've got literally hundreds of people you at least slightly know. Repairing the breach is about cherishing such relationships and treating them like cords on a rope bridge, interwoven with delicacy and skill, until the moment they need to bear some weight, and every single cord is put under pressure and made to do some serious work. If a person is to come back into society after committing a terrible crime, if a family is to be integrated into a neighbourhood having fled from horror and war in a distant land, if a person with profound developmental disabilities is going to become a living, vibrant resident of a housing estate, then all the ropes of the bridge are going to be stretched and tested. A peace curriculum is about raising citizens who know how to make such bridges and have the courage to walk with people across them.

The experience of being taken seriously, of having one's gifts noticed, nurtured, refined, stretched and celebrated should make us people who want to do the same with and for others. The root of the word educate is 'to lead out'. In a dysfunctional household, neighbourhood or society, enormous energies are pent up, ignored, stifled, and never led out by anybody. Repairing the breach means making bridges and forming channels through which people can express the glorious diversity of gifts they've been given, and leading these gifts out in a wonderful human chain of discovery and abundance. There's nothing more exciting than watching a person who has been told for years they're useless find that in fact they have gifts to offer that a community desperately needs and values.

Repairing the breach means learning to heal, building trust, and releasing gifts. Resurrection work; peace work. What Jesus taught the disciples to do in Galilee. What Isaiah wanted his people to learn on their return from exile. The imitation of Christ, who repaired the breach, the breach between us and God and between us and one another; who is our peace.

The word the New Testament most often uses for peace is 'church'. In Ephesians 2.14–22 we discover the full extent of the way Jesus makes such a community of peacemakers possible. Here, in five steps, we find what peace means.

1 Peace means turning difference and tension from destructive forces into creative ones. It means dismantling destructive conflict and hostility and resolving them into simply tension and difference. Ephesians says Jesus 'has made both groups into one and has broken down the dividing wall, that is, the hostility between us' and thus brings us one new humanity. That's what *ubuntu* espouses and the twelve-step process seeks: hostility turned into mutual understanding and mutual understanding turned into active partnership.

2 Next Jesus makes us one body. This is what being bathed in baptism represents and being fed in communion enacts: one broken body making one united body, a body shaped for friendship with God for ever. Peace is not about throwing away the damaged and distressing; it's about restoring and healing the broken and despoiled.

3 Then Jesus gives us one peace – 'peace to you who were far off and peace to you who were near'. In Jesus, so Christians dream, everyone who has trodden the path of reconciliation will recognize themselves – because to be on the way, to be headed through the twelve steps, is to be in Christ. He is what peace looks like.

4 Next, Jesus makes us members of one household. The three Greek letters *oik*, which represent the core of the word for home, appear no fewer than six times in the last four verses of Ephesians 2 – we have 'aliens', 'household members', 'built', 'structure', 'built together' and 'dwelling place', all coming out of the same root of 'home' – *oik*. The same root gives us the words 'economics' and 'ecology'. If in the church Jesus brings us a new identity, a new unity and a new community, then being members of one household shows us how Jesus brings a new politics. That politics believes we are all at different steps in different relationships, personal and corporate, on the twelve-step process of peace. There isn't any other politics. It's all about turning diverse energies from destructive tension and conflict into creative tension and dynamic community.

5 And finally Jesus brings one holy temple, one dwelling place for God. Thus Jesus inaugurates a new identity, a new unity, a new community, a new politics and finally, here, a new worship.

In other words this journey of peace, though we may never have realized it, is, and always was, in the end about worship. Here – through new identity, restored unity, becoming one body, living a new politics, discovering true worship – here we have become the place where others will see the glory of God. We have become church.

CPSIA information can be obtained
at www.ICGtesting.com
Printed in the USA
LVHW042251021221
705152LV00023B/581